THE
POCKET GUIDE
TO

Coffees and Teas

AUTHOR BIOGRAPHY

Founder and executive director of the Coffee Information Institute, Kenneth Anderson is the author of more than twenty books on food, health, and nutrition. He has been the editor of *Nutrition Today* and *Today's Health*, and a vice-president of the Gourmet Society of New York.

THE
POCKET GUIDE
TO
Coffees
and
Teas

KENNETH ANDERSON

A PERIGEE BOOK

Perigee Books
are published by
G. P. Putnam's Sons
200 Madison Avenue
New York. New York 10010

Library of Congress Cataloging in Publication Data

Anderson. Ken. 1921—
    The pocket guide to coffees and teas.

    "A Perigee book."
    1. Coffee. 2. Tea. I. Title
TX415.A5   1982   641.3'372   81-15789
ISBN 0-399-50600-4   AACR2

The Pocket Guide to Coffees and Teas
was produced and prepared by
Quarto Marketing Ltd.
212 Fifth Avenue. New York. N.Y. 10010

Editor: Bill Logan
Editorial Research: Stephen O'Connor
Designed by Ken Sansone
Maps by Steven Kovacs
Illustrations by Abby Merrill

Printed and bound in the United States of America by Maple-Vail
Group.

Table of Contents

PART TWO: TEAS

PART THREE: HERBAL TEAS

ACKNOWLEDGEMENTS

The author would like to thank James Quinn, editor of the *Tea & Coffee Trade Journal*, for his help in obtaining background materials. Thanks too to Joe Kerchelich for contributing some gourmet's ratings.

Special thanks are due to Donald Schoenholt, president of Gillies' 1840 in New York, who provided valuable information about coffee marketing and contributed his expert ratings.

How to Use This Book

This volume serves both as a companion and as a guide for the lover of fine coffees, teas, and herbal teas. The introduction sketches the ancient myth and folklore attending the discovery of the drinks. Each of the three principal sections includes both historical and cultural information, and an alphabetical guide to the gourmet's beverage choices. The sections on coffees and on teas also include descriptions of the implements best used in preparing the drinks. Appendices list both retail and mail-order sources for all items.

The coffees section provides a guide to over 40 unblended coffees, selected and rated by gourmet tasters, and grouped by country of origin. Popular blends receive separate listings. Instant coffees and commercial blends are not considered. Grinders and brewers are not mentioned by brand, but each major type is evaluated.

The buyer's guide to teas is separated into several sections. Among unblended teas, the three types—black, green, and oolong—are listed separately. Blended teas and scented teas each have their own listings. The small number of distinct teas makes it impractical to provide a rated guide, but each tea is exhaustively described in terms of quality, flavor, and aroma. A brief discussion of teapots and paraphernalia evaluates the choices available to the gourmet.

The Herbal Teas section, unlike the previous ones, consists of only two parts: a historical introduction and an alphabetical guide. The wide variety of herbal flavors makes a rated guide impossible, but the flavors and aromas are carefully described. Since many people like to blend their own herbal teas, a repertoire of suggested blends is also included.

Introduction
The Lore of
Infusions

"It quenches the thirst. It lessens the need for sleep. It gladdens and cheers the heart." Is it coffee? Or tea? Or some herbal? The text is from one of the world's first medical books, the *Pen ts'ao*, supposedly written by the Chinese emperor Shen Nung in 2737 B.C. It describes an herb called *t'u*, which may or may not be modern tea, but it could as well describe any of the caffeinated or herbal potions that have been gladdening hearts for centuries. Curiously enough, even in recent times, the introduction of new drinks has depended on an herbal principle like caffeine. Soft drinks— those beverages mothers hate—were originally introduced as health and well-being tonics. Colas, whose appeal comes from the caffeine in the cola plant, were first introduced as "brain and nerve tonic." The original Hires Root Beer was touted in precisely Shen Nung's terms: "soothing to the nerves, vitalizing to the blood, refreshing to the brain." And the mysterious 10,2,4 on old labels of Dr. Pepper bottles refers to the hours at which it was supposed to be drunk for the maximum health benefit.

As exaggerated as such claims may seem, we may imagine that their power is tied to a very basic human delight: the discovery of water that is not only potable but actually tasty and healthy. The practice of boiling water to make it safe to drink is as old as civilization. Archeologists have found hearths in the Dordogne area of southwestern France dating from the heydays of Cro-Magnon and Neanderthal cultures. Broken and discolored pebbles found around the hearths are thought to have been pot-boilers, stones that were heated in the fire, then dropped into a bucket made of wood or hide, boiling the water and splitting the stone.

Though few people boil their coffees or teas today, the instructions for oriental rituals show how important it was to select the right water and carefully boil it in preparing ceremonial infusions. Lu Yu's ninth-century masterpiece—

• •

the *Ch'a Ching*, or *Classic of Tea*—is the Chinese foundation on which Japan's famous tea ceremony rests. In it, Lu Yu warns against well water and against water from a swift stream, which, if drunk too often, can "cause trouble at the neck." The best water, he said, is spring water or water from a slowly moving stream, and all tea water should be boiled three times before adding the leaves. The traditional instructions for the preparation of Turkish coffee, too, specify that the water should be boiled three times.

Of course, boiling the wrong leaf or the wrong bean could well cause something worse than a troubled neck. The prehistory of herbal potions must have been gruesome. Even in modern times, there are enough stories of migrants who, coming to a new country, made tea or salad from a plant that looked just like one they had used at home…with deadly results.

The history of poisons as well as the history of cures is intimately tied to herbals. The longtime resistance to commercial preparations of herbal tea—which has diminished since the 1960s, thanks to several new companies—may in part be due to the traditional association of herbal teas with witch's brews and the mysterious cures that wrinkled old wives used to offer young children.

Even coffee and tea, whose delights have been insisted on for over a millenium, were ritually prepared so as to prove that they were pure. The Japanese tea ceremony presents every step in the making of the tea before the eyes of the guests, including the gathering of the water, its boiling, the cleaning of the utensils, and the addition of the tea. The host wipes the rim of the teabowl before passing it to the guest, and the guest ritually turns the bowl one half turn, sipping from the side opposite that proferred by the host. Arab and Turkish coffee ceremonies are even more aboveboard, since the host drinks first to assure his guests "that there is no death in the pot."

Over the years, hundreds of herbs have proved virtuous, for every sort of disease and sometimes even for help in love. Herbs whose virtues are matched by a palatable taste are described in Section Three of this book, with suggestions for blending them into genuinely delicious drinks. The two giants of the herbal world, however—coffee and tea—have their virtues described in the myths of their origin and progress.

Tea was not just discovered but was miraculously created, when Bodhidharma, the Indian founder of Ch'an Buddhism, tore off his eyelids. He had been meditating before a wall for nine years without pause when his eyes began to close from fatigue. Unwilling to give in to sleep, he removed the offending eyelids. Where they fell there sprouted a bush with shining green leaves that, when properly prepared, have kept the Buddha's disciples alert ever since.

It is little wonder then that Ch'an Buddhists—ancestors of Zen Buddhists in Japan—became regular users of tea, their religious usage forming the basis for the later, secularized Japanese tea ceremony. (For a complete description of the ceremony, see page 105.)

Buddhist monks brought tea to Japan as early as 794 A.D. Indeed, there is one tea plantation in Japan that claims to have been producing the leaves continuously since 815 A.D.! Tea was regarded by both monk and emperor as a divine healing herb, and the royal tea garden was under the jurisdiction of the emperor's Bureau of Medicine.

The drink lost favor in the ensuing centuries, as the emperor's power weakened and the country fell into civil war, but when powerful military clans reasserted the emperor's authority (as their puppet) in the thirteenth century, the monks were again ready to exhibit tea. The fact that the Zen abbot Yeisai was able to cure the dying Shogun Sanetomo, apparently by serving him tea, reestablished the drink as "the divine healer." Neither had it lost its religious use. Keizan, later founder of the Soto sect of Zen, attained religous enlightenment (called *satori*) by shouting, "I drink tea at teatime; I eat rice at mealtime!"

Coffee has no comparable story of its origin, perhaps because a coffee cherry looks more like clotted blood, and a coffee bean more like a rabbit pellet, than like any organ of religious significance. Indeed, in both coffee-discovery stories, the coffee is accidentally consumed, but the result is the same as for tea.

According to one story, Kaldi, the Arabian goatherd, one day came upon his goats standing on their hind legs and bleating, apparently having eaten cherries from a shiny green bush growing in the area. Kaldi, a trusting sort, tried a few himself and was soon dancing with the animals. Some say a Moslem mullah came upon him dancing and scolded him; others say he brought the beans to a monastery, where the monks also scolded him. All agree that the monk's righteous scepticism about the devil's fruit soon turned to delight when they discovered that the drink made from it could help them stay awake for prayers!

The second story is similar. The dervish Omar was driven into the desert with his followers to die of starvation. In a desperate effort to save himself and his friends, Omar had them boil and eat the cherries they found growing on an unknown bush. Not only did the cherries and their broth sustain the exiles, but the survival was taken as a religious event by the citizens of the nearest town, Mocha, who promptly canonized Omar and his beverage, coffee.

From the very beginning, both coffee and tea had the ultimate in herbal virtues: they brought health and well-being, enabling one to stay awake to perform God's work. No wonder the drinks were so well received in early modern Europe. The early explorers, traders, and capitalists all worked furiously doing what they regarded, often quite seriously, as the Lord's work. Beer and wine—the native potations—only stupefied them, while coffee and tea helped them redouble their efforts.

The drinks had additional cachet in Europe, because they were products of the mysterious East. What the Greek historian Herodotus had said about the lands of Araby and Inde still fascinated the Renaissance West. In the land of Inde, by which was meant the Far East, all birds and animals were larger. All the rivers ran with gold, and ants the size of foxes dug it from the ground. Instead of fruit, the trees bore a kind of wool far superior to that vulgarly cropped from lambs. Araby, on the other hand, was "the only country in the world producing incense, myrrh, cassia, cinnamon, and laudanum." Europeans were well disposed to adopt drinks brought laboriously from the Land of Plenty and the Land of Spice.

The Modern Man or Woman, however, had little patience with the elaborate oriental rituals associated with the drinks. (For a complete description of these rituals, see pages 65 and 105.) Ironically, however, Europeans developed their own previously unheard-of array of drinking rituals. There was the obligatory early morning cup, meant to give the drinker a start on the day; the social breakfast cup; the cup of "elevenses," when all England stopped in midmorning for a spot of tea; the after-lunch cup, to aid the digestion and drive off the fumes of midday beer; the afternoon social cup, enjoyed by the women gathered in their parlors, of the formal and informal teas and *kaffeeklatschs;* and, of course, the days and nights of the great cafés and coffeehouses, where business and events were reviewed and hammered out to the rhythm of clinking cups.

Far from outgrowing ritual, the modern temperament has spread it throughout our daily lives. And though today's drinking may often be more informal, it sometimes still calls for paraphernalia every bit as complicated as oriental cere-mony. The French historian Jean-Maurice Biziere notes that "the action of drinking tea or coffee can require the presence of a whole range of cups, saucers, sugarbowls, spoons, teapots, coffeepots, and creamers, all made of the finest, most costly, and most delicate materials, of porcelain, gold, and silver; and the ritual requires, besides, that the table be covered with a fine, clean cloth, like the napkins given to the guests."

Today's drinker of coffees and teas will find a hundred ways to praise it, perhaps in terms close to Shen Nung's, but surely no hymn to the drinks is as moving as that sung to coffee by the beautiful Betty in Bach's *Coffee Cantata:*

"Ah! How sweet coffee tastes! Lovelier than a thousand kisses, sweeter far than muscatel! And if anyone should wish to please me, let him give me...coffee!"

With that apostrophe to launch us, let us consider, one by one, the history, cultivation, and types of coffees, teas, and herbal drinks.

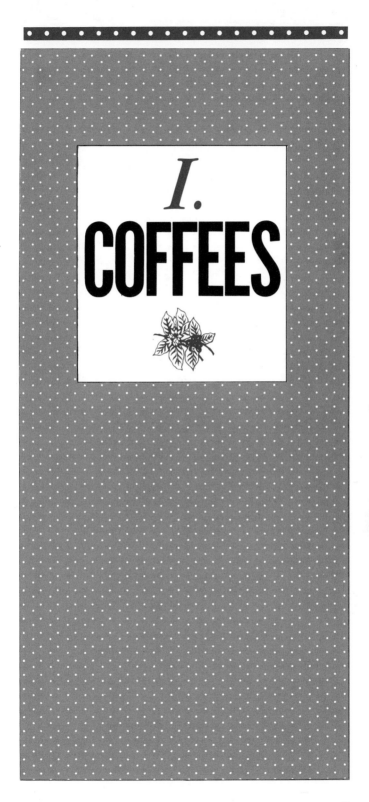

I.
COFFEES

1.
Coffee in History

Coffee's first users did not employ it in a manner too pleasing to modern taste. The Galla tribe, warrior nomads from the mountains of Ethiopia, made a sort of bonbon out of animal fat and coffee beans. During raiding or hunting expeditions, this was their only food. Another tribe, living on the shores of Lake Victoria, favored a porridge made from the beans. Not until Arab traders penetrated Ethiopia in the fifteenth century, returning with the beans that were to become the basis of the great plantations in present-day Yemen and Aden, did anyone get the strange notion that coffee might be used to make a drink.

In fact, the Arabs made two drinks: *kisher* and *bounya*, both known under the generic name of *kahwah*, or *caoue*. *Kisher*, a drink that resembles modern tea, was made from the husks of the coffee cherry. Though it is still drunk with gusto in Yemen, it has never become popular elsewhere. The second drink, *bounya*, spread so far and became so popular —under the general name, coffee—that a nineteenth-century French historian would claim: "The three ages of coffee are the ages of the modern mind."

The Turks were the first foreigners to adopt the Arab drink, importing both the beans and the style of preparation from Mocha. What we call Turkish coffee is really made in the Arab style, purloined by the Turks. The only novelties the Turks introduced were the spices they sometimes added to the black brew: clove, cinnamon, cardamom, or star anise. The Arabs preferred saffron. Spices notwithstanding, the following ancient description of the way to make Turkish coffee holds equally true for Arabian:

They place a small pot on the fire, containing about a cup of water, and when it has boiled they throw in a spoonful of powdered coffee; they then stir the mixture, allowing it to boil and froth a few seconds more, after which all of it— both liquor and grounds—is poured into a cup the size of an eggshell, which itself is mounted in a gold or silver setting which serves to protect the hands from the heat. They sip this liquor when it is nearly boiling—black, thick, and frothy—and it is their greatest delicacy.

• • • • • • • • • • • • • • • • • • •

The late introduction of coffee into countries beyond Arabia was only partly due to the economic and intellectual introversion of Medieval Europe. The Arabians were quite possessive about their *caoué*, guarding the secrets of coffee culture as though they were classified military plans. It was forbidden to transport coffee plants across the borders of the Moslem nations, and the berries of the coffee tree were permitted beyond Arabia only if they had been boiled or dried in the sun to ensure their sterility. It wasn't until the year 1600 that fertile coffee seeds were first smuggled out of Arabia and carried to India by a Moslem pilgrim named Baba Budan. (The descendants of those trees were found growing in a mountainous area of Mysore earlier in the twentieth century.) The spread of coffee culture thus began—as it would continue—with a theft.

Europeans learned about the existence of coffee nearly 40 years before they had a chance to taste it. One of the earliest published reports about coffee to be read by Europeans was written by a German physician and botanist, Leonhard Rauwolf, who traveled in the Orient and the Levant from 1573 to 1576. In the Middle East, Rauwolf claimed, the people consume "a very good drink they call Chaube that is almost as black as ink and very good in illness, especially of the stomach. This they drink in the morning early in open places before everybody, without any fear or regard, out of clay or China cups, as hot as they can, sipping it a little at a time."

In 1592, another European botanist mentioned an Arab infusion called *coava*, and Captain John Smith—later better known for his relationship with the Indians of Virginia, Pocahontas in particular—encountered the beverage on his

The original Arabian coffee vendor, like his later imitators, needed considerable acrobatic skill.

Arabian travels at about the same time. It wasn't until the early seventeenth century, however, that coffee began to make commercial inroads in Europe.

Enterprising Venetians began importing Arabian beans as early as 1615, and soon had a clientele of influential aristocrats. The Dutch, meantime, became the first Europeans to succeed at removing a live coffee plant from Arabia, thus laying the foundation for the subsequent Dutch coffee industry in Java. The basis for the Mocha Java blend, mainstay of the coffee connoisseur right through the nineteenth century, was established by the second decade of the seventeenth century.

Coffee did not enter Europe unopposed, however. The Dutch had been drinking cocoa for more than half a century, and had recently introduced tea, as well. The market for exotic drinks, thought some merchants, might well be glutted.

The infant coffee industry also ran into trouble with the Roman Catholic Church. Because coffee was a Moslem beverage, priests petitioned Pope Clement VIII to forbid coffee-drinking by Christians. While hearing claims that coffee was an invention of the Devil, the Pope asked for a sample of the beverage of Satan so he could examine it personally. According to the story, Pope Clement sipped a cup of coffee and declared the drink "so delicious it would be a pity to let the infidels have exclusive use of it." According to legend, the Pope then baptized the coffee to make it a truly Christian beverage. With papal approval, coffee grew in popularity in Italy. Not only did the nobility drink it at home, but it was sold by street vendors called *aquacedratjos*, who also offered lemonade and chocolate drinks.

In France and Austria, too, coffee was peddled from house to house throughout most of the seventeenth century. The sellers must all have been something like Candiot, the first coffee vendor in Paris who, according to one authority, wandered the *rues* "wrapped in a white apron, carrying before him a pewter tray with all the implements necessary for making coffee. In his right hand he carried a small heater with a coffeepot, and in his left, a pitcher full of water to fill the coffeepot at need. He went from street to street in this outfit, crying in a loud voice, 'Coffee!' " He and his type would serve you the drink at home, from his cups or your own, for only two sous, sugar included if you wished. When sales were slack, as they often were before the general public had taken an interest in coffee, the vendors could survive on the other delicacies they often sold: lemonades and pickled cherries, strawberries and nuts.

Coffee-drinking in Europe, however, flourished mainly in private homes, at first among the families of diplomats or businessmen who had experienced ritual coffee ceremonies on visits to the Middle East. A Monsieur de la Roque of Marseilles, for example, accompanied the French ambassador to Constantinople and returned with a complete Turkish coffee service, including cups, embroidered napkins, and a quantity of coffee. Coffee-drinking was also practiced in Europe by students, clergymen, and those who had been

• •

born in Turkey, Lebanon, or other Middle Eastern countries. The diary of John Evelyn in 1637 notes that the former Bishop of Smyrna was the first person observed drinking "coffey" on the campus of Oxford University.

But in the second half of the seventeenth century, a transformation began that would make coffee one of the most popular drinks in Europe. The coffeehouse—meeting place of bankers, dissidents, artists, merchants, poets, wits, plotters, and plain rogues—was in some ways the cradle of modern Europe. Coffee changed, in less than a century, from the drink of a few princes and a few paupers to the chief social beverage of the rising middle class. The direct agents were usually commoners who had lived in the East or skilled servants brought back from Araby by European merchants. Theirs were the first coffeehouses.

Coffeehouses had long been a tradition in Moslem countries. Many were famous, with names like Cafe of the Gate of Salvation, and important businessmen and government representatives felt obligated to visit them during their travels. The Moslem coffeehouses often featured jugglers and musicians, and, like the European coffeehouses that followed, those in the Middle East tended to become hotbeds of political activity. To discourage too much political talk, a sixteenth century Shah of Persia placed mullahs in the coffeehouses with instructions to sit daily discussing ecclesiastical law, poetry, history, and other, less controversial, subjects. The Grand Vizier Kuprili of the Ottoman Empire was not as subtle about controlling coffeehouse political discussions. Coffeehouses were ordered closed and patrons of illegal coffeehouses were given a beating if caught. On a second offense, they were to be sewn inside a bag and thrown in the ocean.

Europe offered a virgin, and perhaps safer, market for men like Pasqua Rosee, founder of some of the first coffeehouses in the West. Rosee was brought to London by Daniel Edwards, a merchant who traded with the Middle East, for the purpose of preparing and serving coffee for Edwards and his friends and family. But the coffee attraction in the Edwards home drew too much company and, recognizing the business potential, Edwards helped Rosee establish a coffee preparation-and-service business for the public in a tent (or shed) in St. Michael's Alley, Cornhill. The original coffee tent eventually evolved into a substantial house financed by Rosee's partner, a coachman named Bowman. Rosee, whose venture helped spawn a segment of history and thousands of English coffeehouses, left England to start coffeehouses in Holland and Germany.

The establishments sprung up throughout Europe in a similar manner, often opening first in seaports such as Venice and Marseilles before moving to the inland capitals. In one case, however, the Turks did the importing themselves.

In 1683, the soldiers of the Ottoman Empire, having recently overrun Hungary, advanced by the hundreds of thousands against the city of Vienna. Among the defenders of the besieged city was Franz George Kolschitsky, a Pole who had lived for some years among the Turks, acquiring their ways and customs. He disguised himself as a Turk and slipped through the enemy lines to deliver a message to the relief force approaching Vienna. Legend has it that Kolschitsky was detained briefly by a Turkish leader who, mistaking him for a wayward soldier, hospitably offered him a cup of coffee.

Legends aside, the Pole did reach the relief force, and the Christian troops soon stood overlooking the besieged city. One of the captains, amazed, later wrote to his wife that the Turkish camp seemed at first sight to be as big as Warsaw and Lemberg put together. Its size could not help it in the decisive battle. The relief troops swept down on the camp while the city's defenders sallied out from behind their walls; the Turks fled in disorder, leaving their whole camp intact on the field.

The victors found all kinds of outlandish goods among the spoils, including parrots, monkeys, and 500 huge sacks of an unknown "dry, black fodder." Men were burning the odd-smelling fodder when Kolschitsky walked by, noting the odor of roasting coffee. He put a stop to the burning and returned to the city, knowing at last what boon he would ask as a reward for his valor. The city awarded him all the beans plus a shop in Vienna from which to sell the drink he claimed he could make from them.

The brew—black and full of grounds, as the Turks like it— did not appeal to Viennese taste. To promote the drink, Kolschitsky decided to filter out the grounds and cut the flavor with milk and honey. His was perhaps the first coffee served with milk for any but medicinal purposes. Offered with crescent rolls or doughnuts, it made his shop a huge success. Soon, Vienna could boast over 100 coffeehouses, all inspired by his example.

All over Europe, the founding of coffeehouses increased demand for the beverage. In England, 13,000 kilograms (28,600 pounds) of coffee were imported between 1699 and 1701. A survey conducted around 1700 found some 2,000 coffeehouses operating in London alone. One of the famous old coffeehouses, Garway's, also became the first establishment in England to sell cups of tea to the public. Hot chocolate drinks also became available at about the same time, even though both chocolate and tea had been introduced in private homes before coffee. The demand for coffee was so great that coffeehouse keepers prepared the beverage in 10-gallon urns. The brew was served in a dish rather than a cup and the price was two pence per dish.

In addition, the London coffeehouses usually required a one-penny cover charge, paid upon entering. The patron placed his penny on the bar and, while he received no coffee for his penny, the charge did pay for the privilege of listening to the debates and discussions by the intellectuals who frequented London's coffeehouses. The price also included the right to read the newspapers purchased by the coffee-house keeper and access to the lamps that provided illumination for reading.

The discussions of current events, religion, politics, and economics were so profound, or at least so ubiquitous, that coffeehouses were known as penny universities. They also were sometimes called seminaries of sedition, since they helped spawn novel political notions that challenged the authority of the crown. One group that met in coffeehouses to discuss liberal political views was identified by Samuel Pepys as the Rota Club, because the members favored an annual rotation of the members of parliament. The coffeehouses usually set aside tables for discussion of various topics and the table frequented by political agitators was often known as the treason table.

In December, 1675, hoping to prevent the kind of ferment that had so recently cost James I his head, King Charles II issued a proclamation for the suppression of coffeehouses, to become effective January 10, 1676. The proclamation aroused such a public outcry that it was recalled on January 8, two days before it was to become effective.

Charles was not the only one upset by the popularity of coffeehouses. Polemics sprang up everywhere over the health effects—good or ill—of coffee. The highlight of the debate was a petition from a group calling themselves the Women of England, in which they called on their men to "reject that Drying, Enfeebling Liquor, a poison which would make them as unfruitful as those Desarts whence that unhappy Berry is said to be brought and to forbear to trifle away their time, scald their crops and spend their money for a little base, black, thick, nasty, bitter, stinking, nauseous Puddle Water."

Most of the political, mercantile, and intellectual leaders of the time meant, by example, to prove the Women wrong. Among the English wits who regularly met at their favorite coffeehouses were Samuel Johnson and Boswell, Goldsmith, Burke, Adam Smith, Sir Joshua Reynolds, Hogarth, Defoe, Chatterton, Fielding, and Addison. A bit of coffeehouse gossip was the basis for Alexander Pope's "The Rape of the Lock." Scientists such as Francis Bacon and Dr. William Harvey, who is credited with the discovery of blood circulation, were also coffee enthusiasts. Indeed, a coffee club founded by students at Oxford evolved into the Royal Society.

Given the way the wits preferred their coffee, however, one might be tempted to side with the Women. They liked their brew clear and black, without a bit of grounds. To achieve this end, they usually added to the pot a bit of fish skin (sole or eel) and some egg white or eggshell. Though this procedure was not supposed to affect the flavor, it should be noted that they often drank the coffee with a dash of port, possibly in self-defense.

Among the long-range social effects of the London coffeehouses was the introduction of the practice of tipping waiters. Many of the coffeehouses featured brass-bound boxes that were inscribed with the words To Insure Promptness. Patrons were expected to drop coins in the boxes for the coffee servers and other members of the coffeehouse staff. Of course, the initials of the inscribed words formed the now common acronym, tip.

English coffeehouses may have been the liveliest in Europe, but the French cafes excelled them in elegance. The French ones have also survived and prospered while the English ones have disappeared. Paris's famous Cafe Procope just off the Boulevard Saint Germain has been open continuously since the 1680s, though today it is a restaurant. The tastefully mirrored walls and marble-topped tables of

Coffee was a frequent peace offering in the Old West.

● ●

the Procope, so often imitated since, were not, however, the original style of French cafes. The first ones could be found not in Paris but in Marseilles, where they had a relatively unsavory reputation as tough hangouts. And even then, the usual controversy over coffee-drinking swirled through the country. A duchess warned her friend to avoid the drink, describing how the Princess of Hanau died in horrible pain on account of the "hundred little ulcers" in her stomach caused by drinking coffee. A Marseilles medical student was even more specific:

The irritating parts in which [coffee] abounds are so subtile and so quick-moving that, spreading through the mass of the blood, they first bring on serosity in all the other parts of the body. From there, they attack the brain, after having dissolved all the humidity of the greater corpuscles, and they keep all the pores wide open, preventing the animal spirits that cause sleep from rising to the brain, while at the same time blocking the pores; thus it happens that these irritating parts cause one to stay awake so long that the nerve fluids whose force is necessary to revive the spirits completely disappear, and the nerves relax, causing paralysis and impotence; and because of the sharpness and dryness of this thoroughly burned blood, all the limbs become so bereft of fluids that the whole body is made horribly gaunt.

Such hysterical warnings did little to stem the drink's growing popularity in France. The founding of cafés like the Procope made the coffeehouse a respectable place to congregate, and the leading figures of the Enlightenment came out in force. Within a few years, poets would be writing odes to coffee, claiming "It's you, sweet coffee, whose liquor tart/ turns not the head but swells the heart."

Looking back on France's great century of the Enlightenment and the Revolution, the historian Michelet saw the growth of the modern nation reflected in French coffee-drinking habits. Before 1700, he said, coffee was an exotic delight imported from Araby for the great ladies of the Court. But within a decade, the French were bringing coffee from their own colony, the island of Bourbon, making it far cheaper. "This coffee," writes Michelet, "grown in volcanic earth, occasioned the explosion of the Regency and of the new spirit, the sudden hilarity, the laughter of the old world, that torrent of sparks of which the light verse of Voltaire and the *Persian Letters* give us but the faintest idea."

Michelet's third coffee, that brought from Martinique and Santo Domingo, brings on France's maturity: "That strong coffee—plain, spicy, nourishing as well as stimulating—fed the adulthood of the century, the strong age of the *Encyclopedia*. It was drunk by Buffon, by Diderot and Rousseau; it added its fervor to fervent souls, its light to the penetrating sight of the prophets gathered in the "den of the Procope" who saw at the bottom of the black brew the ray of the revolution to come."

The eighteenth century saw European coffee consumption expand at a rate beyond the merchants' wildest dreams.

England alone, which imported almost 13,000 kilograms (28,600 pounds) of coffee at the turn of the century, imported 200,000 kilograms (436,000 pounds) of the beans during a comparable period around 1773. That was a sixteen-fold expansion. Meanwhile, the reexport trade had grown over 400 times its previous size! Some monarchs tried to prohibit coffee; others, like Frederick the Great of Prussia, simply decided to tax it. Frederick hired a squad of "coffee-smellers" to ferret out illicit brewers of contraband beans.

Without nearby monarchs to suppress the drink, the New World quickly embraced it. The London Coffee House, which was in existence in Boston in 1689, may have been the first European-style coffeehouse in the New World. Coffee by the drink was available to the public in America prior to 1689, but only in taverns that dispensed other forms of liquid refreshment as well.

Coffeehouses were instrumental in the growth of American commerce and the progress of the American Revolution. The Merchants' Coffee House in New York City was so well known by 1758 that people gave directions by referring to the distance and direction of a given destination from the coffeehouse. Colonial patriots mourned the "Interment of their Liberty" as a result of the Stamp Act of 1775 by covering even the backgammon boxes at the Merchants' in black and the dice in crepe. The letter calling for the First Continental Congress was written at the Merchants' and, after the revolution, Alexander Hamilton and his friends created the Bank of New York there.

The British Stamp Act of 1765 and the tea tax of 1767 led to a general boycott of tea in the English colonies and a greater appreciation for coffee, even though coffee beans cost the equivalent of five dollars a pound in an era when a good meal was priced at 12 cents. Ships from England carrying tea were not permitted to dock at some American ports. And, of course, the Boston Tea Party in 1773 became a turning point in the competition between coffee and tea as the breakfast beverage for Americans. Coffee was declared the sovereign drink of American colonists, a prejudice that evolved into a tradition.

One Boston coffeehouse-tavern, the Green Dragon, was dubbed by Daniel Webster the headquarters of the American Revolution. (Although the Green Dragon was also frequented by some colonial officials, crown officers, and red-coated British soldiers, the loyalists had their own favorite coffee-house, called the British.) It is said the Boston Tea Party was planned in the Green Dragon, where John Adams, Paul Revere, and other patriots of the Revolution met for coffee and political discussion. As the outbreak of hostilities approached, patrons of the Green Dragon and the British met in increasingly frequent street brawls. But when the revolt finally came, it was at another Boston coffeehouse, the Bunch of Grapes, that the Declaration of Independence was first read to the public. In the celebration that followed, the coffeehouse was nearly destroyed by a bonfire built in the street.

Coffee spread from aristocracy to middle class in the

● ●

eighteenth century; in the nineteenth it spread to the work-ing class. Coffee with milk came into its own, not as a social beverage but as a cheap and nutritious breakfast. Sugar was also added, though the correct drinker specified that the sugar should be placed in the cup first. Fresh, hot coffee should then be added, and stirred until the sugar had dissolved. Only then was it permissible to add the milk.

Some English drinkers went a step further, cutting out the water altogether. Coffee milk was made by adding a spoonful of coffee to cold milk, then cooking the concoction for a quarter of an hour. Regretably, fish skins were also common additions to this drink.

The advantages of coffee with milk, taken in the morning, were well summarized by the French gourmet Brillat-Savarin: "A cup of coffee well laced with milk will not hinder your intelligence; on the contrary, leaving your stomach free of rich foods, it will not tire your brain....Soon the suave molecules of Mocha will stir your blood, without unduly heating it; the organ of thought will feel a sympathetic force; work will become easier, and you will feel well right up until the main meal which will restore your body, and give you a calm and delicious evening."

2.
Cultivation and Commerce

Coffee woke modern Europe to consciousness of itself, encouraging industry and commerce, startling men out of ale- or wine-induced stupors. The coffee tree itself was just as startling to European science. A flowering evergreen that bears both blossoms and fruit several times each year, often simultaneously, was a novelty to early botanists. Flowers, with a scent so sweet and pungent it was often wafted several miles out to sea from coastside plantings, combine with both ripe and unripe cherries on the same branch.

Classical mythology, much admired in the Renaissance, identified Arabia with scents and spices. Theophrastus had commented, "In Syria and Araby, the earth itself gives off a sweet odor, and all that is produced in these countries has a pleasant smell; everything there is hot and dry, and nothing rots." Perhaps misled by the popularity of such notions and relying mainly on its heady perfume, Antoine de Jussieu, a noted French botanist and curator of King Louis's Jardin des Plantes, called the flowering coffee plant a member of the jasmine family.

The great eighteenth-century naturalist Linnaeus corrected him, giving the plant a genus of its own, *Coffea*. Although over 100 species of *Coffea* have since been discovered, only a few are used to make the black brew called coffee. The most sought-after species—*Coffea arabica*, or *arabica* for short—grows to a height of about 6 meters (20 feet) or more in the wild. On modern plantations, it is kept to a height of about 1.5 meters (5 feet), more convenient for pruning and picking. The flowers are white and when, after two or three days, they fall, they carpet the ground with delicate petals. The clusters of cherries, or berries, that contain the bilateral bean start green, gradually turning a deep, rusty red.

Arabica trees, and their less desirable cousin, *robusta*, must grow for five to seven years before the cherries are first ready for picking. This fact helped encourage a seven-year

● ●

boom-and-bust cycle, since a spate of new plantings in one year would inevitably result in a glut of beans five to seven years later. As a result, growers in Colombia have recently developed a fast-growing species, the *caturra*, that is shorter-lived than *arabica* but that matures more quickly.

Other experiments involve pruning older trees back almost to the roots. New growth produces beans within a year. *Arabica* trees may live for a century, but they are in their prime between ages seven and fifteen. The average tree can produce 5 kilograms (10–12 pounds) of cherries each year, but this amounts to only 1.5 kilograms (3–4 pounds) of husked and washed beans.

The commercial history of coffee cannot be reliably traced before the fifteenth century, when Arabs are known to have operated irrigated coffee plantations in Ethiopia, selling the harvest to coffee merchants in cities across the Red Sea. But documents suggest that coffee was being cultivated in either Yemen or Ethiopia, or perhaps both, nearly a millenium earlier.

The early coffee farmers transplanted wild trees from the highlands of Ethiopia, but later they learned how to grow coffee plants from seeds, carefully starting the trees in nurseries. The young trees were placed in holes, about 1.5 meters (5 feet) deep, dug into the slopes of hills where mountain streams could be diverted to provide the abundance of moisture the plants required. Shade trees were planted alongside the young coffee trees where necessary to protect the coffee plants from the burning sunlight.

Sunlight, however, helped process the ripe fruit after it had been harvested: the ripe coffee cherries were spread over the open ground or left on the trees to dry, making it possible to remove the pulpy husk that surrounds the bean.

Remarkably, some of the basic procedures for producing coffee have changed very little over the centuries. In many parts of the world, particularly the areas of Arabia where coffee cultivation began, coffee trees are still grown on terraced hillsides, shaded where necessary by other trees. Even in regions such as Hawaii where coffee cultivation is a relatively new industry, some of the ancient techniques are used. Hawaiian coffee growers dig deep holes in the volcanic rock of mountain slopes as sites for new trees. The holes resemble giant outdoor flower pots, with soil and gravel packed around the roots to trap and hold moisture. Also in the centuries-old manner of the Ethiopian coffee growers, some producers today spread the freshly picked coffee cherries on the ground or paved terraces to dry them before removing the fruity pulp from around the bean.

Not all coffee producers use the sun-drying technique. Some growers, particularly those with large plantations and large supplies of water, soak the cherries overnight in huge vats or float the cherries in sluices that terminate at pulp-removing machines. The water softens the outer skins of the cherries, which makes the pulping process easier. Coffee cherries that are soaked in water are sometimes called *washed* and those that are sun-dried are identified as *unwashed*. Unwashed does not mean the same as unclean, and, perhaps in self-defense, producers of unwashed coffees often prefer to use the term "natural" to describe their way of removing the husks by drying rather than wetting the skins. The washing procedure, however, does make it easier to control fermentation and, thus, the final taste.

Some growers, especially in Brazil, still allow the cherries to dry on the trees. In fact, there are customers who demand coffee beans from cherries that have dried on the trees: the bitter flavor that results is claimed to be an integral part of the taste of New Orleans style coffees. And some buyers insist on beans that have been produced through the primitive procedure of drying in the sun. Still, the majority of the world's coffee drinkers find the taste of the tree-dried beans, called rioy, rather unpalatable.

Wherever coffees are produced, and by whatever method, there are a few constant requirements that assure the proper growth and fruiting of the coffee tree. And, not unexpectedly, the trees that yield the finest coffees are the trees that are most sensitive to changes in climate and geography, and most susceptible to disease. The climate must include average minimum temperatures of 12°C (55°F) and average maximum temperatures of about 25°C (80°F). One frost will destroy a crop; a deep frost will destroy the trees. Water must total approximately 1.75m (70 in.) a year; too much will ruin the crop, but too little may kill the trees. And the moisture must be evenly distributed throughout the year. A few hours of sunshine are needed every day, but no more than that. Mountain slopes in tropical regions help control the amount of sunlight because the sun is partly hidden by the peaks, and the clouds often provide additional shading, particularly during the hot, humid periods. The soil must be rich, moist, and in a layer several feet thick atop a porous, rocky subsoil that drains excess moisture. Africa, Latin America, and the larger mountainous islands in tropical or subtropical latitudes generally meet these requirements. They lie within a belt that extends about 30 degrees north and south of the Equator, the region that is the source of virtually all of the world's coffees.

THE CARIBBEAN

All of the *arabica* trees in the world today, except those of Africa and Yemen, are descended from a single tree, one stolen by Gabriel Mathieu de Clieu in 1723 from the royal Jardin des Plantes in Paris. The tree had been a Dutch gift to Louis XIV, and de Clieu, inspired by the Dutch success with growing coffee in their island colony of Java, decided that the French should have a coffee industry in their own West Indian possessions. With the help of the royal physician and a masked gang, de Clieu broke into the Jardin des Plantes one night, stole the royal coffee tree, and smuggled it onto a ship headed for Martinique. The tiny tree was nearly destroyed by salt water during a storm at sea. When fresh water was rationed, de Clieu shared his daily portion with the tree.

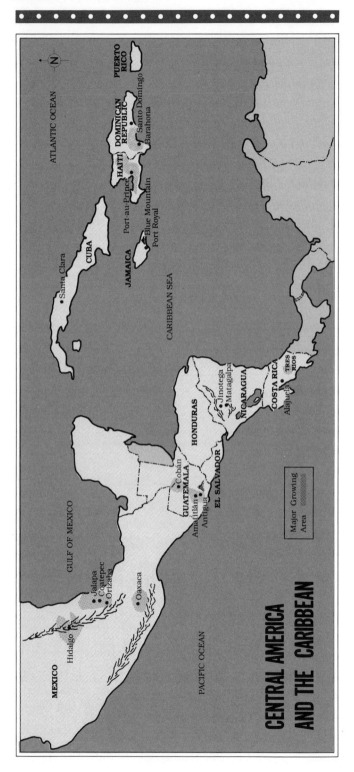

CENTRAL AMERICA
AND THE CARIBBEAN

Major Growing Area

MEXICO
Hidalgo
Jalapa
Coatepec
Orizaba
Oaxaca

GUATEMALA
Cobán
Amatitlán
Antigua

EL SALVADOR

HONDURAS

NICARAGUA
Jinotega
Matagalpa

COSTA RICA
TRES RIOS
Alajuela

CUBA
Santa Clara

JAMAICA
Port-au-Prince
Blue Mountain
Port Royal

HAITI

DOMINICAN REPUBLIC
Santo Domingo
Barahona

PUERTO RICO

ATLANTIC OCEAN

GULF OF MEXICO

CARIBBEAN SEA

PACIFIC OCEAN

N

• • • • • • • • • • • • • • • • • • •

Arriving in Martinique, he planted the coffee tree in his garden, concealing it behind large thorn bushes. The stolen tree survived, producing its first crop of coffee beans three years later.

By the end of the eighteenth century, there were more than 18 million coffee trees on Martinique alone. Today, Martinique is no longer an important source of coffee. Unable to compete with the burgeoning industries of Cuba and Puerto Rico, Martinique converted to sugar and tobacco. Coffee beans that appear in stores under a Martinique label were most likely grown on Guadeloupe and transhipped through Martinique. Other islands of the Greater and Lesser Antilles have fared better in recent years as suppliers of fine coffees. Jamaica is most notable, with its Blue Mountain and High Mountain types ranking among the world's best beans.

However, the Martinique coffee plants proved to be the fountainhead for all the modern plantations of Central America, Latin America, and East Asia. The Caribbean islands dominated coffee markets for a century beginning in the mid-1700s. Martinique, Cuba, Puerto Rico, Haiti, Jamaica, the Dominican Republic, and Guadeloupe were all major producers. Competition from the new Brazilian coffee industry, together with the improved availability of Mocha and Java beans, sent the Caribbean coffee plantations into a decline in the middle of the nineteenth century from which they never recovered. Though Caribbean coffees are still fine in quality, they are now usually scarce.

Jamaica produces some of the world's finest coffees, but only in small quantities. Professionals joke that Brazil exports more coffee in a weekend than Jamaica does in a year. They are not far wrong. Trade in the famous Blue Mountain coffee is controlled directly by the Jamaican government, and amounts to only about 20,000 bags per year. Most of the crop goes to Japan, whose popular *koohi shoppus* (coffee shops that are really more like fancy cafés) can afford to pay the 13 dollars per pound or more that the roasted beans cost wholesale. Other excellent Jamaica coffees are grown by one large private corporation and by a cooperative composed of small, independent growers. Their coffees, too, are restricted in availability.

The rest of the Caribbean area exports just as little coffee today. Cuba, once a major exporter, now sends coffee mainly to Eastern Europe, although small amounts are sometimes available in France. Puerto Rico produces only enough for the home market. Haitian and Dominican coffees are sometimes found abroad, but they are relatively scarce. The commercial blends made to appeal to Cubans and Puerto Ricans in the United States contain no coffees from Cuba or Puerto Rico.

• • • • • • • • • • • • • • • • • • •

CENTRAL AMERICA

In the western hemisphere, almost all commercial coffee production is found below the Tropic of Cancer, the northernmost crops coming from the *altura*, or mountainous

A branch of the coffee tree. Each coffee cherry (D, E) contains two coffee beans (F).

Mexican regions of Hidalgo and Vera Cruz. Mexican coffee production began in Vera Cruz around 1800, with the transplantation of trees from the West Indies, and gradually spread westward through Oaxaca to the Pacific Coast slopes. But Vera Cruz coffees, particularly the Coatepec, Jalapa, and Huatusco types, have dominated the Mexican coffee market for most of its history.

The coffees of Central America profit from the area's steady climate and wealth of mountains. The mountains of the Pacific Cordillera, which stretch in a virtually unbroken line from Guatemala to the middle of Panama, provide the best combination of climate, altitude, and soil.

Guatemala was a relative latecomer to the commercial coffee business, exporting beans only since 1875. The mountainous country is ideally suited for coffee production and exports now surpass those of much larger countries. The best known of the Guatemalan varieties are Coban and Antigua. Before World War II, Germany bought more than half the annual Guatemalan coffee crop. European merchants still take about 50 percent of the Guatemalan beans, with most of the best beans today being exported to England.

Today, Germany depends upon El Salvador as a source of Central American beans. In fact, most of the better coffee beans of El Salvador are exported to European markets. The United States is a good customer, but mainly for the low-grown, acidy grades that are used for commercial blends.

Honduras produces coffees that are similar to those grown in the neighboring countries of Guatemala and El Salvador. And, like the coffees of the neighboring Central American countries, most of the annual crop is shipped to European coffee merchants.

Costa Rica began growing coffee more than 200 years ago, using plants transported by Spanish colonists from plantations in Cuba. The little Central American country has pioneered in many areas of quality coffee production. Costa Ricans invented and developed the modern machinery used to husk and wash coffee beans, machinery that helps the producer control the fermentation—and thus the final flavor —of the beans. Costa Rica became perhaps the first Latin American country to sell its entire export crop to a European country, through an arrangement with a British merchant who agreed to serve as an agent for the Costa Rican producers if they would sell the annual harvest on the London market. For nearly a century, most of Costa Rica's coffee was exported to Europe.

Located between Costa Rica and Colombia, Panama should be a leading producer of high-grade coffees. For some reason (perhaps because its economy is tied up in the Panama Canal) it is not. Panama grows only a small amount of coffee, most of which is either consumed domestically or sold in Europe. The exports amount to a few thousand bags per year, compared to millions of bags by other Central American countries.

SOUTH AMERICA

In terms of the manpower employed in its production, coffee is the largest agricultural commodity in the world today. The huge coffee industries of Latin America, especially of Brazil, are mainly responsible. Brazilians were still drinking imported coffee while the Dutch, French, and Spanish were developing coffee plantations in their Caribbean and Latin American colonies. But a Brazilian military officer, Francisco de Melo Palheta, put Brazil in the coffee business with a deed even more daring than de Clieu's burglary of the Jardin des Plantes. Both France and Holland had established colonies along the northeast coast of South America and the northern border of Brazil, and both were developing coffee plantations along a disputed boundary. Brazil was asked to arbitrate the boundary controversy.

Brazil sent Palheta to French Guiana to help resolve the dispute. According to several reports, Palheta spent quite a long time on the project because the surveys and border inspections were frequently interrupted by visits with the wife of the Colony's governor. When the land surveys were completed, the governor's wife presented Palheta with a large

SOUTH AMERICA

Major Growing
Area

bouquet as a token of the colony's (and her own) appreciation. Although it was forbidden, on penalty of death, to allow coffee seeds or plantings to be removed from the French plantations, Palheta's bouquet contained cuttings of young coffee plants—which became the cornerstone of Brazil's massive coffee industry.

It was 1727 when Palheta left Cayenne, French Guiana, with his bouquet of coffee cuttings and a handful of seeds. Within a few days, he had planted them near Para, Brazil, at the mouth of the Amazon River. Five years later, Brazil was in the coffee business. From Pará, coffee cultivation spread southward through the states of Maranhão and Bahia, and by 1770 coffee trees were growing in Rio de Janeiro. Catholic clergy, too, helped establish the coffee industry in Brazil in the eighteenth century, planting seedlings around monasteries and convents. Today, coffee is grown throughout Brazil, but most of the commercial coffee production is confined to a few states bordering the South Atlantic: the area from Bahia south to Paraná.

Most commercial plantations are located on plateaus that range in altitude between 600 and 1250 meters (2,000 and 4,000 feet) above sea level and are exposed to temperatures that average 14°C (60°F) in the winter and 22°C (72°F) in the summer. However, varied patterns of harvesting and processing have evolved in different areas of Brazil over the past two and a half centuries. Some trees seem to produce continuously, with flowers, green cherries, and ripe cherries on the branches at the same time. Other trees may suddenly flower simultaneously over tremendous areas, carpeting miles of Brazilian landscape with small white flowers.

The one-day flower show is followed by an equally simultaneous ripening of coffee cherries on millions of trees and the recruitment of all able-bodied persons in the area to bring in the harvest. Brazils, as Brazilian beans are called, can be of high quality, but Brazilian coffee growers usually try to produce a huge amount of coffee beans and quality is a secondary consideration. Often, both ripe and unripe beans are stripped from the tree, resulting in a coffee of uneven flavor.

Colombia, even more than Brazil, is ideally suited for coffee-growing. Located at the northwestern corner of South America, Colombia has direct access to both Atlantic and Pacific shipping lanes. Its seaports are at the mouths of rivers that extend hundreds of miles inland like watery highways, winding among the mountain slopes and plateaus that support coffee farms. The soil is a mixture of humus and ancient volcanic rock particles, combining fertility with excellent drainage. The climate is so consistent that accurate forecasts can be printed a year in advance. (To find a change of climate, Colombians merely drive to a different elevation above sea level.) At the elevation of most coffee plantations, between 750 and 1,850 meters (2,500–6,000 feet), the temperature averages approximately 20°C (70°F) all year round. The constant weather guarantees a consistent pattern of blooming, fruiting, and harvesting, resulting in a predictably excellent coffee.

Colombia lagged behind Brazil as a commercial coffee producer by nearly a century, acquiring its first trees from the French Antilles through neighboring Venezuela around 1800. The first exports of Colombian coffee were recorded in the mid-1830s. But Colombia today is the leading producer of high-quality *arabica* beans. Nearly 30,000 Colombian farms and plantations produce an annual export crop of approximately 10 million bags. The Colombian types— Medellíns, Armenias, Manizales, Bogotás, and others—yield flavors and aromas that assure almost immediate consumption of each year's harvest. While favored as new-crop beans, Colombians also age gracefully and rank with aged Sumatras and Javas as the world's finest vintage beans. But old-crop Colombian beans are scarce because of the demand for the beans before they have a chance to age.

A less publicized source of South American coffees is Venezuela, which in some years produces and exports as much *arabica* coffee as Costa Rica or Nicaragua. Though lesser known, the best Venezuelans are among the world's best coffees. Venezuelan coffees are often identified simply as Maracaibos, named for the principal seaport through which the beans travel to the outside world. Maracaibos can include the Cúcuta variety grown in Colombia but shipped through Maracaibo because it is the nearest seaport. Particularly prized are Mérida and Caracas beans. Venezuela has been in the coffee business since 1784, when a priest started a small plantation near Caracas with seeds that he had brought from Martinique.

Another little known but important South American producer of *arabica* beans is Peru, which supplies the United States, its main customer, with approximately half of its annual crop of nearly 45 million kilograms (100 million pounds). The better beans of Peru, often identified simply as Peru coffees, are grown on the slopes of the Andes Mountains in the northern part of the nation. The Chanchamayo Valley, in the southern interior, is also a major producing region. Coffee has been produced in Peru for many years, but mainly for domestic consumption; the country's entry into the export market is relatively new but promising.

Other coffee-growing countries of South America include Bolivia, Ecuador, and the former European Guianas, now known as French Guiana, Surinam, and Guyana. With the possible exception of some coffees grown in Ecuador, none of the crops is commercially important and the coffees of Ecuador are not really distinctive.

AFRICA AND ARABIA

As Africa assumes an increasingly important role in world coffee production, the gourmet shopper is likely to find new choices in specialty stores. Many of these African coffees have only been available since the 1970s. Curiously, although the world's *arabica* coffees all came originally from Ethiopia, and today all Latin American and Caribbean coffee is made

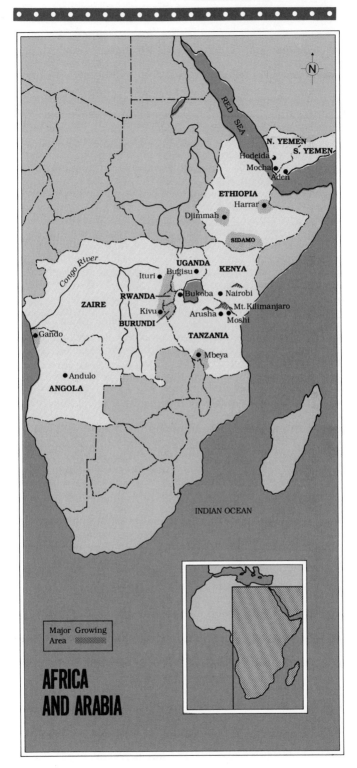

N

RED SEA

N. YEMEN

S. YEMEN

Hodeida

Mocha

Aden

ETHIOPIA

Harrar

Djimmah

SIDAMO

Congo River

UGANDA

Ituri

Bugisu

KENYA

ZAIRE

RWANDA

Bukoba

Nairobi

Kivu

Mt. Kilimanjaro

BURUNDI

Arusha

Moshi

Gando

TANZANIA

Mbeya

Andulo

ANGOLA

INDIAN OCEAN

Major Growing
Area

AFRICA
AND ARABIA

• •

from *arabica* beans, about 75 percent of Africa's coffee consists of beans of the *robusta* species.

The *robusta* bean is native to Africa, too, but the relatively recent boom in its culture is due to economic, not natural, factors. Since they are more disease resistant and higher yielding than *arabica* beans, *robusta* beans are more profitable to grow. They are the preferred source for many commercial blends and especially for the huge, instant-coffee market. Like a cheap whiskey, they are effective if not exactly tasty: high in caffeine, although not distinctive in flavor.

Angola, the Ivory Coast, and Uganda are the major producers of African *robusta* beans. Commercially important, these countries are among the five largest coffee-producing nations in the world, ranking behind first- and second-place Brazil and Colombia. Each of the African countries grows between three and four million bags of coffee annually; much of the yearly crops of *robusta* beans is destined for commercial roasters in America. Still, some of the world's finest *arabica* is grown in Africa. The gourmet should simply make sure that any "genuine African" coffee is also a genuine *arabica*.

Angola produces a small amount of *arabica* coffee of good quality. It may be identified by its source, either Andulo or Gando. The Ivory Coast does not export an *arabica* coffee, but Uganda produces an *arabica* that may be called Bugisu, after the district in which it is grown.

Other African countries that export both *arabica* and *robusta* beans include Burundi, Cameroon, Tanzania, and Zaire. The finest Burundi *arabica* is a rich, high-grown coffee with high acidity. About two-thirds of the Cameroon crop consists of *robusta* beans, but a small portion of the delicious *arabica* may reach the counters of specialty shops. Tanzania grows several hundreds of thousands of bags of fine *arabica*, and a smaller amount of *robusta*, coffees annually. The *arabica* may be identified as Mount Kilimanjaro or Plantation Bukoba. The buyer should make certain that a Tanzanian Bukoba is identified as a Plantation Bukoba, because Bukoba is also a district that produces much of the country's *robusta* coffees. Zaire exports about one million bags of coffee annually. Most of its coffee harvest is of the *robusta* species but the country is also the source of two very fine *arabica* types, Kivu and Ituri, named after the high-elevation districts where they are grown.

The three African countries that grow only *arabica* beans are Ethiopia, Kenya, and Rwanda. The Rwanda crop is small, amounting to only a few hundred thousand bags per year, and the top grades are exported to European dealers. Some of the lesser (but still quite good) Rwanda *arabica* beans are sold in the United States.

Ethiopian coffees are of particular interest because they come from *arabica* coffee's native habitat. They may be the pungent, winey wild beans harvested by local villagers from direct descendants of the trees that bore coffee beans before humans discovered their use, or the smooth but equally ancient Mocha-like Harrar from carefully cultivated plantations. The Harrar beans (called longberry) appear large and

• • • • • • • • • • • • • • • • • • • •

long compared to the small and scruffy-looking wild coffee beans (called shortberry). Even the wild beans from the boondocks, sometimes identified as Djimmah or Sidamo after their growing and marketing areas, are likely to be more tasty than a less-than-best *arabica* from most other coffee-producing countries.

Kenya got a very late start in commercial coffee production, with first plantings early in the twentieth century. However, Kenya coffee growers were able to benefit from the centuries of experience of other countries, and only the Colombians can match the Kenyans for technical innovations. One Kenyan experiment consists of bending young trees over so that eventually the treetops and branches send out roots. The tree becomes its own trellis, increasing yield and making beans easier to pick. Nearly all of Kenya's top grades of coffee beans are snapped up by merchants in Europe, but a few thousand bags make their way to American specialty shops each year.

A different species of coffee, called *liberica*, is grown in the West African nation of Liberia. The annual production amounts to perhaps 100,000 bags and the quality is somewhere between a run-of-the-mill *arabica* and a high-grade *robusta*. Most of the crop is exported to Scandinavia and other European markets.

Once, almost all the *arabica* coffee drunk in the West came from Yemen. Today, little remains of the plantations that made the name Mocha a household word. The port of Mocha has been closed for over a hundred years, and Yemeni exports have declined in recent years to only around 50,000 bags annually. The Yemeni civil war and the consequent division of the country into two parts has reduced exports still further. Now, no Mocha at all comes to us from South Yemen, and only a small amount comes from the North.

• • • • • • • • • • • • • • • • • • • •

INDIA AND CHINA

Today, the major coffee producer of Asia is India, which harvests about one and a half million bags of *arabica* and *robusta* beans annually. The proportions of *arabica* and *robusta* are approximately 50 percent each, and about half of the annual production is exported. The U.S.S.R. is India's best customer. The best of India's coffees are called plantation coffees and the finest of these comes from the Nilgiri Hills. The bulk of India's *arabica* crop is grown in the state of Karnataka and is often labeled as Mysore coffee. A coffee of good quality is grown in Yunnan Province, in southern China, and is beginning to enter the export market, but in very small quantities. Imports of Chinese coffee into the United States, from 1979 through 1980, totaled less than 900 bags.

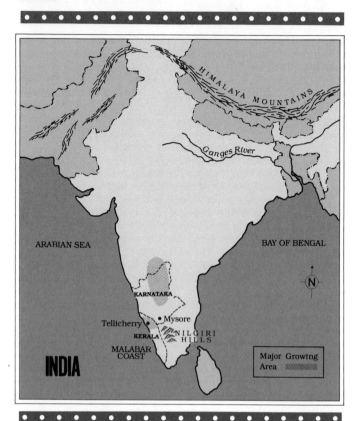

SOUTHEAST ASIA AND HAWAII

The Dutch East India Company had instituted coffee cultivation in Ceylon by 1658, expanding the operation to Java at the end of the century. Coffee thus entered Southeast Asia, and a legendary type was born. Until the end of the nineteenth century, only Mocha could rival Java in the estimation of gourmets, and the two coffees were sometimes combined into the famous Mocha Java blend. Especially prized were the so-called Old Government Javas, beans that developed an inimitable musty character after the five months they spent at sea in the holds of wooden ships.

Faster sea transport meant the end of the Old Government Javas, but far more devastating to the burgeoning coffee industries of the Far East was a leaf plague that struck the coffee plantations of Java, Sumatra, India, and Ceylon in the third quarter of the nineteenth century. All of the region's fine *arabica* trees were wiped out. It was, in fact, this sudden demise of the competition that allowed Brazil's young coffee industry to grow as rapidly as it did.

When Southeast Asia was replanted in the twentieth century, about half of the new plantings were *robusta* trees. At the higher elevations, however, a new strain of *arabica* was introduced. Most of these plantations were seriously

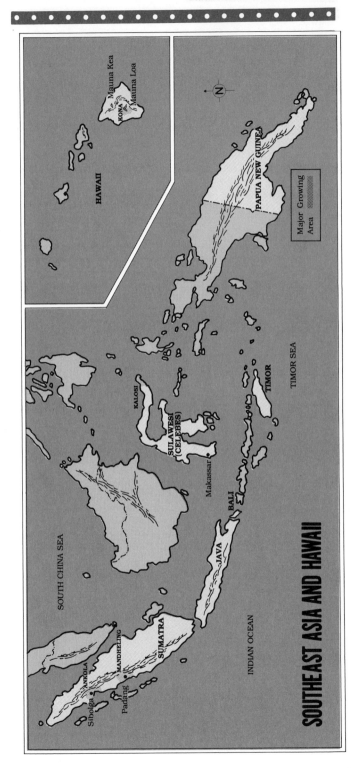

SOUTHEAST ASIA AND HAWAII

Major Growing Area

SOUTH CHINA SEA

INDIAN OCEAN

TIMOR SEA

PAPUA NEW GUINEA

TIMOR

KALOSI

SULAWESI (CELEBES)

Makassar

BALI

JAVA

SUMATRA

MANDHELING

ANKOLA

Sibolga

Padang

HAWAII

Mauna Kea

KONA

Mauna Loa

N

● ● ● ● ● ● ● ● ● ● ● ● ● ● ● ● ● ●

damaged during World War II, but they have recovered strongly since then. Today, these *arabica* beans are among the most prized in the world. Although Java is no longer the area's largest or finest producer, other Indonesian islands—including Celebes (Sulawesi), Timor, and Sumatra—export scarce but desirable coffees.

The Hawaiian coffee industry is small but extremely efficient. Coffee is grown on small plots, averaging only about 2 hectares (5 acres) per grower, in pits carved out of the volcanic rock on the saddle between the Mauna Loa and Mauna Kea volcanoes. This coffee, called Kona after the region in which it is produced, is one of the finest and scarcest in the world. Unfortunately, growing Kona is becoming less and less profitable. Some of the farm families, the descendants of the original Japanese and Portuguese cultivators, are drifting away to serve the tourist industry. The Dutch company that controls some of the plots is converting to an even scarcer and more lucrative crop, macadamia nuts. Kona's fortunes are thus unsure at best.

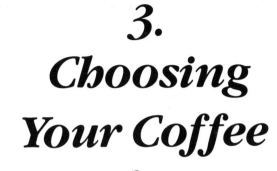

3.
Choosing Your Coffee

I f everybody liked the same kind of wine, there would be only one kind of wine," as the saying goes. The same rule applies to coffee. For people who prefer the convenience of purchasing a can or jar of coffee that has been manufactured for a mass market, with a flavor and aroma designed to satisfy average taste buds, there are commercial blends so similar that consumers readily surrender last week's loyalty for this week's coupon special.

But if you are a coffee lover with discriminating taste buds, the chances are that you want to experience the tastes of unblended and blended coffees made from freshly roasted beans with names like Barahona and Blue Mountain, Coatepec and Djimmah, Kona and Kilimanjaro. When you serve coffee to friends, the beverage may be prepared from the fruit of trees that grew in Sumatra or Kenya, or from trees in Yemen that are descendants of plants that flourished in the region when it was ruled by the Queen of Sheba. Coffees with such pedigrees cannot often be found on a supermarket shelf, but they are available in specialty food shops and from mail-order merchants (see Appendix).

THE GOURMET RETAILER

Tea often comes in airtight tins marketed by companies with centuries-old traditions, but most gourmet coffees are sold by bulk under names given to them by the retailer. It is therefore important for the novice taster to find a coffee retailer whose recommendations can be relied on. Finding such a relationship is certainly easier in large cities where there are many retailers, but any shopper should check that the gourmet retailer satisfies the following basics.

How is the coffee stored and presented? Wooden barrels look authentic, but if they are not relatively airtight, they will allow the coffee to get stale very quickly. Roasted beans left exposed to the air at room temperature for a week and a half will go rancid. When the beans are contained in covered barrels or other receptacles, does each container have its own cover? A surprising number of stores try to cover four or five bins with a single, hinged lid. The result, of course, is that all the coffees are exposed to four or five times as much air. Closed, individual receptacles are best.

If you are unsure about a dealer's reputation for fresh coffee, buy a small amount of a type whose taste you are familiar with. If the taste disappoints, the reason is likely to be that the beans are stale. But if your dealer usually serves you well, be tolerant of occasional lapses.

The way coffee is marketed makes it difficult for the retailer to provide unblemished service. Most retailers buy their beans from roasters who, in turn, buy raw coffee in lots (called chops) of 250 bags each. In almost every chop there are a few bad bags, with diseased, substandard, old, or badly processed beans. The best roasters test beans from every bag, discarding bags whose beans are unacceptable, but such a procedure is very expensive. Consequently, some lesser coffee may get through to the retailer, still labelled as the best. The amount of bad beans is pretty small, however, so if you get a bad batch more than once or twice a year, it may be time to consider shopping elsewhere.

Coffees at a bona fide gourmet shop are not likely to be actually mislabelled, but there are certain labelling conventions to be aware of. House blends may be wonderful or horrible. The ideal house blend should mix a fine, expensive coffee with a less well known or cheaper but very compatible coffee, the combination making a blend less costly than the finest component but equally tasty. In practice, some shops simply throw the leftovers into the house blend, or stock a house blend that is inferior to the rest of their coffees, though not much cheaper. Ask your dealer what the specialty of the house contains. If he doesn't know but the price is attractive, try a little bit and see.

Another convention consists of labelling coffees according to their styles. Thus, there are numerous Blue Mountain Style, Mocha Java Style, and Kona Style coffees on the market. As genuine coffees, all three are quite scarce and sought-after. The term "style" on the label means, of course, that the coffee in question is not the real thing at all, but rather some coffee that a taster has concluded tastes like the famous original. Although the taste-alike coffee may be quite good, it is not apt to be either as good or as scarce as the original. It should not, therefore, carry a price as high (or nearly as high) as the original. If the cost is reasonable, you may well want to try such a coffee, but start with a small quantity to find out what it is like.

Be aware, too, that a dealer who seems to have mainly high-priced dark-roasted coffees is suspect. Many excellent dealers offer fine dark-roasted coffees as well as budget-priced dark roasts. While it is true that any fine coffee will reveal its quality whether it is roasted light or dark, it is also true that lesser coffees will lose their defects the darker they are roasted. Indeed, it is the charred, caramelized flavor associated with dark-roasted beans that their devotees admire, not so much the taste of the bean itself. A tasty, dark-roasted coffee can thus be made from fairly cheap beans, so you should not pay the price of a scarce coffee simply to get your cup of continental, French, or Italian roast. If the dark roast is expensive, find out why. It may be that it is made with an exquisite bean, like Kona, in which case you will have a real treat in store.

There is one rule to follow absolutely, regardless of the store you shop in: Never buy more than you can drink within a few weeks. Keeping beans in a closed container in the freezer may prolong their freshness for up to two months, but no method can preserve them indefinitely. The beans may be as much as five or six weeks out of the roaster when you buy them, so it is not a good idea to tempt fate by buying a quantity that will sit around for another five or six weeks at home.

Very few dealers today roast their own beans, so the buyer is usually dependent on the quality of work of the supplier. If you want to see and smell operations where the roasting is still done in-house, however, visit Schapira's (117 West 10th Street) or Gillies 1840 (160 Bleecker Street) the next time you are in New York City, or the Graffeo Coffee House (733 Columbus Avenue) when you are in San Francisco.

THE FLAVORS OF BEANS

The flavor of your coffee depends in large part on the characteristics of the beans from which it is made—on the species of the bean, how and where it was grown—and how it was harvested and processed. The buyer's guide on page 42 describes the flavor of the coffees you are likely to encounter in specialty stores. A glossary explaining the terms used by professional tasters appears on page 39. There are, nonetheless, some general factors affecting coffee flavor.

Although there are about 100 species of the genus *Coffea*, only four are used to make the drink we call coffee. Almost all of the coffees sought by gourmets are of the species commonly called *arabica*. These coffees are comparatively low yielding and flourish at higher altitudes, but their flavor is easily the most complex and delightful. The hardier and higher-yielding *robusta* and *liberica* strains are high in caffein but low in flavor. They should seldom be seen in a gourmet shop. The *robusta* beans betray their presence in the cup by foaming slightly and sometimes by leaving a tarry ring. In recent years, the Colombians have developed a dwarf subspecies called *caturra*. It matures much more rapidly than an ordinary *arabica* plant, but has a shorter mature lifespan. It was created mainly to break the economic cycle linked to the five-to-seven-year period it takes before a newly planted *arabica* is ready for its first harvest. In the past, a profitable year meant that everyone would plant new *arabica* trees, and the new beans would glut the market exactly five to seven years later. A staggered introduction of the faster-maturing trees means a more even spread of the increased supply. The *caturra* beans now account for about a third of

Colombia's annual production, and in flavor they are the equal of other Colombian beans.

Just as important as species to the quality of coffee are elevation and climate. Here is where the grades that the wholesale dealers sometimes give to coffees can come in handy. Designations like supremo, excelso, AA, and jumbo specify the size and uniformity of the beans being offered. Since uniform size is important to correct roasting, such grades do have meaning for the gourmet. The size of a bean does not generally affect the taste. Gradings that refer to the elevation at which a bean is grown or to the hardness of the bean are more meaningful. Designating a bean as high grown or strictly hard should mean that the bean has been grown at the optimum elevation of 700 to 1,850 meters (between 2,000 and 6,000 feet) and in the best soil for it to develop a fine flavor. The two designations really go together, because a hard bean is usually high grown. A hard bean is not only more flavorful, but it will also roast more evenly, liberating its full flavor potential more consistently.

Different countries use different grading systems, and some fudging of the grades may occur at the retail level. It is therefore best to consider grading information together with other information about a coffee before deciding on its probable quality. Take the Costa Rican grading system, for example. From best to worst, it includes strictly hard bean, good hard bean, hard bean, medium hard bean, high-grown Atlantic, medium-grown Atlantic, and low-grown Atlantic. Thus, a "high-grown" Costa Rican coffee may not be the very best Costa Rican grade. The smart buyer, however, will note that Costa Rican coffees are generally excellent (see Buyer's Guide, page 42) and might take a chance on a coffee described as high grown Costa Rican.

Species and grade can be good general guides to a coffee's quality, but no pedigree will help if the coffee has been improperly harvested. Even with the utmost care, however, not every season's crop will produce equally healthy beans. The ripeness of the beans when they are picked is extremely important, and the methods generally employed to pick the beans will influence the quality of the coffee. A bean that has been picked before it is ripe may look fine after it is roasted, but it will have an unpleasantly sharp or herbaceous flavor.

Some crop-to-crop and tree-to-tree variation cannot be avoided, but growers who strive for quantity above all else will often end up including a noticeable proportion of unripe beans in a given sample. The Brazilians, for example, pick beans by stripping whole branches, despite the fact that coffee beans can mature at very different rates, even on the same branch. Most Colombian coffees, on the other hand, are still picked manually by skilled laborers who select only the ripe beans for plucking. In Jamaica, the pickers don't start work until local bats descend on the trees to suck the coffee cherries, thus indicating that they are ripe.

The processing necessary to remove the skin and pulp of the cherries from the bean also affects flavor. The ancient dry method, called unwashed today, specifies that the cherries be spread in the sun until the skin and pulp wither and can be removed. This process can produce fine coffee, but it is difficult to control. If the beans are packed too close together or if air circulation is insufficient, they may ferment beyond acceptable levels, producing a sour flavor referred to as rioy by tasters. Some gourmets prize this flavor, but most agree that it is unpleasant.

The modern wet method, which results in beans called washed, controls fermentation and thus reduces the chances of getting a rioy flavor. Such washed beans have their skin and pulp removed mechanically, but the remaining pulp is removed by soaking the beans in tanks. They are then dried to stop further fermentation. The designation washed bean on a label, then, will guarantee coffee of a more consistent quality than that called unwashed.

PROFESSIONAL TASTER'S GLOSSARY

The following are terms used by professional coffee tasters to identify the flavor characteristics of coffees. They appear frequently among the entries in the Buyer's Guide section, beginning on page 42.

Acidy. A sharp and pleasing taste that is neither sour nor sweet. An acidy coffee has snap, sharpness, a lively taste. It does not necessarily indicate the actual degree of acidity in the bean. Acidy coffees are mainly produced in Colombia and certain other Latin American countries.

Aged. Coffee beans that have been stored for one year or more before roasting. They have lost their acidy characteristics, becoming instead richly sweet and heavy bodied.

Body. A taste sensation experienced as heavy or thick as the flavor settles onto the tongue. It is accompanied by a richness of flavor and aroma. A coffee that lacks flavor and aroma will usually lack body as well.

Caramel. A caramel flavor produced by chemical changes in the carbohydrates in the coffee bean when exposed to roasting temperatures of around 204°C (400°F).

Groundy. A musty, earthy taste associated with coffee that has been damaged in drying or storage.

Harsh. An unpleasant taste, reminiscent of raw weeds, and characteristic of *robusta* coffees and Brazils that have been allowed to dry on the tree. It should be noted that a few coffee drinkers prefer harshness in the cup (see Rioy).

Hidy. A coffee that has absorbed the aroma of leather or animal hides as a result of being stored or shipped in close proximity to these items.

Musty. A term usually applied to coffee flavors that result from improper heating or drying during processing. However, there also is a mustiness in vintage coffees that is a preferred quality. Gourmets, for example, love the naturally sweet mustiness of vintage Colombian coffee.

Rioy. A harsh, medicine-like flavor present in some coffees produced in the Rio district of Brazil. The term is sometimes applied to any harsh-flavored coffee. The heavy, somewhat pungent, taste is preferred by a few coffee drinkers in the southern United States and France.

Tannin. An astringent flavor characteristic caused by the presence of chemicals that are related to tannic acid. A similar characteristic is found in teas and certain red wines.

● ●

COFFEE ROASTS

The flavor of a bean is determined by many factors, but its flavor and aroma are brought to life by roasting, during which virtually odorless green coffee beans are exposed to temperatures of between 204-260°C (400–500°F) for a period of about five minutes. Dark roasts can be produced by holding the beans in the roaster for a longer time or by adjusting the temperature. The roasting process triggers chemical reactions that can continue for days or weeks after the roasting is completed. The chemical changes eventually lead to staleness unless the roasted beans are frozen or packed in an airtight container to prevent oxidation of the volatile chemicals created by the roasting process.

A darker-roasted bean tends to have an oily surface because the longer exposure to high temperatures forces oils within the bean to the outside. The darker color is the result of carbonization of cellulose and caramelization of starches and sugars in the bean.

A century ago, almost all roasts were dark. Coffee usually was roasted in the home or by the retail merchant who had his own small, batch roaster. Coffee roasting at home was something like popping corn in the fireplace. Green beans were placed either in a cylindrical drum attached to a long rod that was turned by hand, or in special heavy skillets that rested directly in the hot ashes. Some of the devices were known as coffee burners, which suggests the condition of the finished beans.

Commercial coffee roasting was done in a similar manner, an obvious difference being that the big processors used large-scale equipment and were somewhat more delicate about the degree of roasting. A large barrel holding up to 75 kilograms (175 pounds) of green beans was loaded by a husky man who also had to turn a crank while the beans roasted in the furnace for about 30 minutes. When the smoke coming from the barrel turned a certain shade of gray, the barrel was removed from the furnace and the beans, some of them burnt by the 1093°C (2,000°F) heat, were dumped on a stone floor to cool.

Modern roasters have made possible a variety of roasts, each of which can lend its particular flavor to any coffee.

The guide below lists the various kinds of coffee roasts offered by gourmet and specialty shops.

After-Dinner Roast. A coffee that has been roasted to a dark, but less than very dark, brown color. It has a somewhat oily surface. An after-dinner roast lends a bittersweet, tangy flavor to the beans.

American Roast. A coffee that has been roasted to a medium-brown color, with a dry rather than oily surface. An American roast is acidy, but also noticeably sweet and rich in flavor. It may also be labelled as regular roast, but is usually labeled as American roast because it is particularly favored by American coffee drinkers, who are notorious middle-of-the-roaders.

Cinnamon Roast. The lightest of the standard coffee-roasting categories. The finished surface is light brown and dry. A cinnamon roast has a distinctively sour flavor. Because of its popularity in the northeastern United States, a cinnamon roast may also be identified as a New England roast. It does not contain cinnamon.

City Roast. A medium-dark roast, slightly darker than an American roast but not as dark as a full-city or light French roast. A city roast lends a neutral taste, lacking the acidy characteristics of American roast and the tang of darker roasts.

Continental Roast. A dark-brown roast with an oily surface. It has more tang than a city roast and definitely lacks the acidy taste of lighter roasts. It may also be listed as a dark roast, French roast, or Italian roast.

Dark Roast. See Continental Roast.

Dry Roast. Not a true roast, but a method whereby the freshly roasted beans are allowed to cool slowly in the surrounding air, as opposed to the usual method of quenching the hot beans with water. Air drying does not significantly affect flavor.

Espresso Roast. A very dark roasted coffee that is preferred for the fine grind required for espresso coffee-making equipment. An espresso roast results in a very oily, black bean. The taste of the carbonized cellulose dominates any natural aroma or flavor that may have been in the bean. *Robusta* beans are sometimes used in very dark roasts: *robusta* beans can only be improved in flavor by the intense roasting, whereas the heat drives out the volatile flavor factors present in an *arabica* bean.

French Roast. See Continental Roast.

Full City Roast. A coffee roast found mainly in the New York City area where coffee drinkers prefer their beans roasted to a degree that is just noticeably darker than a regular city roast and with a bit more tang. It may also be called high roast.

Heavy Roast. A dark-brown to nearly black roast with a surface that is even oilier in appearance than espresso or continental roast. A heavy roast is completely devoid of acidity, and its tang is all but overwhelmed by the carbonization and caramelization of the carbohydrates in the bean.

High Roast. See Full City Roast.

Italian Roast. A coffee that has been roasted to a degree that is darker than a high roast. The surface of the bean is dark brown and oily but not as dark and oily as a continental roast. An Italian roast is the type most popular with consumers in the coffee-producing countries. It has the rich coffee tang of a dark roast, unconcealed by the taste of carbon.

Light Roast. See Cinnamon Roast.

Light French Roast. A medium- to dark-brown roast marked by spots of oil on an otherwise dry surface. It is comparable to a regular city roast in aroma and flavor.

Medium Roast. See American Roast.

New England Roast. See Cinnamon Roast.

Summer Roast. Coffee roasted in a warm, humid atmosphere to reduce the bean's sweating. Sweated coffee, as it is also called, has a darker brown color after roasting than it would if it had been roasted under low humidity. Green coffee beans may be given a steam bath before roasting in order to increase the degree of brown coloration. This procedure improves appearance, but has little effect on flavor.

● ●

THE GOURMET BUYER'S GUIDE

The coffees listed in this section are virtually all made from *arabica* beans, but each has a distinct flavor and aroma. An explanation of the technical terms sometimes used to describe flavors will be found in the Taster's Glossary on page 39. To further help the buyer, our consultants—all expert tasters—have classified the coffees as follows:

******	Outstanding	***	Very Good
*****	Excellent	**	Good
****	Unusually Good	*	Fair

● ●

UNBLENDED COFFEES

Angola. Though it is a huge producer of *robusta* coffees, Angola also exports a small amount of *arabica*. Rather flat by itself, Angola *arabica* can be a good partner in blends. Angola ***

Blue Mountain. See Jamaica.

Brazil. Brazil is the world's largest producer of coffee, all of it *arabica*. The emphasis on quantity means that even the best Brazilian beans are not usually of top quality. Bourbon Santos, named for the French colony where the ancestors of the Brazilian bean once grew, makes a smooth and palatable beverage; it is not distinctive enough to either excite or offend discriminating taste buds. Although Brazil's unpredictable weather causes the bean to vary in quality from crop to crop, it is usually reasonable in price. The combination of mild flavor and inexpensive cost make it the ideal weak partner in a blend. Coffee called Paraná, for the region in which it is grown, is comparable in quality. Brazil's other coffees, especially those of the Rio type, are harsher, sometimes even acrid. Remarkably, Rio coffees were the main coffees imported into the United States up to the turn of the century. Bourbon Santos *** Parana *** Rio *

Burundi. All the 300,000 bags of coffee produced annually in this African nation is of the *arabica* type. The coffee is full-bodied and acidy. Most of it goes to the United States. Burundi ****

Cameroon. Less than half of Cameroon's crop is *arabica*, but what there is has a mellow, sweetish flavor. Since peaberry and elephant beans—coffee mutants attractive for their size and shape—are sold separately, lovers of those mutants are the most likely to find themselves buying Cameroon beans. Cameroon ****

Celebes. The modern name of this island in the Indonesian group is Sulawesi, but its coffees are still known collectively by the island's former name, Celebes. Most Celebes coffee goes to Europe, but small amounts are available in the United States. Kalosi is so full-bodied it is almost syrupy, but it also has a sharply acid tang. The coffee called Boengie is similar, but with a smoother, spicier flavor. Kalosi **** Boengie ****

Chagga. See Kenya.

China. China's own coffee, often called Yunnan for the province in whose mountains it is produced, is available in a few stores in the United States. It makes a rich, full-bodied, lightly acid brew, with a touch of the sweetness found in old-crop Indonesian coffees. Yunnan ***

Colombia. This Latin American country is the second largest producer in the world (after Brazil) but it is first for quality. Once it was possible to buy a wide array of Colombian coffees with names like Bogotá, Bucaramanga. Giradot. Honda, and Tolima. Today, the government has rationalized production, selling most Colombian coffee under the acronym MAM, which stands for the growing centers of Medellín. Armenia. and Manizales. Although coffees sold under the acronym may come from any of these Andean-foothill regions, each region has distinctive characteristics. Medellín is the best: rich, full-bodied, and mildly acid. Armenia is a bit thinner in the cup and somewhat less acidy, but still quite full-bodied with good aroma and a touch of the winey flavor of true Mocha. Beans from Manizales make for a rich, winey brew, with greater acidity but less body than Medellíns and less subtlety than Armenias.

Because the best Colombian beans are hand-sorted, the grading system is also important. Beans labelled supremo are all of the largest size, uniform and without imperfections. This means that they not only look nicer in the grinder, but they roast evenly and uniformly. The grade excelso means that the bag contains a mixture of supremo, medium-sized (or extra), and peaberry beans, all without imperfections. Perfect peaberries may also be sold separately, for devotees of those rounded mutants.

A rare treat is Vintage Colombian, a coffee made from beans that have been stored in warehouses for up to eight years before roasting. In the interval, the acidy characteristics of the coffee are replaced by a pleasantly sweet, almost syrupy richness. Since Colombian coffee is in demand from the day it is harvested, very little is held in storage. Medellín ***** Armenia **** Manizales **** Vintage ******

Costa Rica. Costa Rican coffees are the strongest in flavor of all the Central American varieties. Some gourmets adore them, while others remain unmoved. In general, Europeans are fond of their sharply acid, heavy-bodied flavor. Their detractors claim they leave a slightly too pungent aftertaste. The very best Costa Rican beans come from the highest elevations of the mountains on the country's Pacific side. One such comes from Alajuela, yielding a hearty brew whose mild but sharply acid flavor has the snap of a very dry wine. Costa Rican ***/****

Dominican Republic. Haiti and the Dominican Republic share one island (Hispaniola), but they produce different coffees. The Haitian coffee has a more distinctive flavor, but most feel that the Dominican is more pleasant. Like good Central American beans, Dominicans produce a rich, moderately acid cup of coffee. The full-bodied Barahona is the best Dominican coffee, particularly suited to dark roasts because its flavor survives the long roasting. Coffee labelled Santo Domingo is similar in flavor, but it may be pleasantly sweet. Barahona **** Santo Domingo ****

El Salvador. This mountainous country is a source of *arabica* coffees comparable to those of neighboring Guatemala. The quality of coffees from El Salvador, as in many other producing countries, improves with the altitude above sea level of the producing farm or plantation. Coffees from this Central American nation that are grown above 1,200 meters (4,000 feet) are enjoyed for their mild, somewhat sweet taste and medium acidity. However, they lack a distinctive flavor or aroma. Those grown at lower elevations, sometimes graded as Central Standard (as distinguished from High Grown) tend to be less full-bodied and more acidy. El Salvador ***

Ethiopia. Some say that coffee takes its name from the Kaffa region of Ethiopia, which may be the native home of the *arabica* bean. Some Ethiopian coffee still grows wild in the Djimmah, Sidamo, and Kaffa areas, where it is picked and sun-dried by the local populace. Beans sold as Djimmahs betray their wild origin: they are small, irregular, and generally ugly. Gourmets who prefer all-natural products enjoy the earthy, spicy flavor and the slightly pungent aftertaste of Djimmah.

There is some disagreement about the virtues of Djimmah, but none about the coffees of Harrar. Sometimes known as Harrar longberry or Ethiopian Mocca, the bean is indeed a close relative of true Mocha and, like its relative, it is carefully cultivated. The Harrar bean yields a liquor that is as deep in color as claret. Its flavor is strong, winey, thick. Indeed, because it is so pronounced in flavor, it is an excellent choice for the strong partner in a blend. Try matching it with Colombian or mild Central American beans. Djimmah ******* Harrar ********

Guatemala. Guatemalan coffees are distinguished by their almost smoky flavor and their high acidity. The very best are grown in the high-mountain regions of Antigua, Amatitlan, and Cobán. The Cobán is sometimes almost bitter. Note, too, that Guatemalan beans may not look exactly pretty. The Antiguas, especially, tend to split during roasting, but their rough appearance does not spoil their fine flavor.

The giant *arabica* coffee bean Maragogipe is produced in all parts of Guatemala. Because it grows better at lower elevations than other *arabica* varieties, the Maragogipe coffee tree is usually cultivated in lowland areas and its beans should not be expected to equal the flavor of high-grown coffees. Antigua ******** Amatitlan ******* Cobán ******** Maragogipe ****/*****

Haiti. Haitian coffees usually have a rich, mildly sweet flavor, with moderate acidity. Those that are unwashed, including the Port-au-Prince variety, may have a pungent aroma and aftertaste. Because the Haitian beans make a fine dark roast, most are sold to French and Italian dealers. Haitian *******

Harrar. See Ethiopia.

Hawaii. Coffee is produced mainly on the slopes of the Mauna Loa volcano, from trees transplanted from Brazil. Almost all of the coffee grown is called Kona, named after the region where the trees are cultivated on numbers of small farms resembling open-air greenhouses. The trees are planted in holes chopped out of the volcanic rock and nurtured with soil and fertilizers brought from elsewhere. All this labor produces a unique coffee, very full-bodied and very sweet. Moreover, the sweetness is neither syrupy nor cloying. Mark Twain, who had traveled all over the world by the turn of the century, commented: "I think Kona coffee has a richer flavor than any other, be it grown where it may and call it what you will." All Kona is outstanding but the finest, graded Kona 1, contains only large, perfect beans. Kona **********

Honduras. Coffee from this Central American nation is light-bodied, mild, and moderately acidy. Although inoffensive, it is not particularly distinctive. Honduras ******

India. The British buy most of India's coffee exports. The most commonly seen variety is Mysore, grown in the state of Karnataka (formerly Mysore) in southern India. The coffee is quite dark and full-bodied, but it is only slightly acidy. Although the British love it, others often find it dull. A better Indian coffee is the richer and more delicate Malabar, grown in the Nilgiri Hills. Mysore ****** Malabar *******

Jamaica. High-grown coffees from Jamaica are the finest in the Caribbean and among the finest in the world. The famous Blue Mountain beans grow on the slopes of the 2,251-meter (7,388 feet) mountain of that name, in plantations controlled by the Jamaican government. The roasted beans yield a mellow, aromatic brew, mildly acid and quite full-bodied. The whole effect is as delicate as broth. Blue Mountain coffee is one of the rarest coffees in the world.

Other Jamaican beans are scarce but not rare. Jamaican High Mountain coffee is grown in the Blue Mountain region on land owned by the giant Salada Tea Company. Four times as much acreage is devoted to the growing of High Mountain as is devoted to Blue Mountain, so the former is not quite so rare. Flavors are comparably excellent, although devotees of Blue Mountain detect more delicacy in their favorite. Jamaican Mountain Choice coffee is the name for coffees grown by a cooperative of small farmers. Their beans, too, are excellent, when you can find them. The most commonly seen Jamaican coffee is called either Prime Washed or just Jamaican. Though it is a fine, mellow coffee in itself, it is not the equal of its scarcer compatriots. Blue Mountain ****** High Mountain ***** Jamaican Mountain Choice ***** Prime Washed ****

Java. The name Java is practically synonymous with coffee, but today's Java coffee is not the same magnificent beverage it once was. A plague during the 1870s wiped out the trees originally planted by the Dutch, and World War II decimated the later replacements. Moreover, the 20 weeks it once took to ship Java beans to the West has now been reduced to 11 days, so the beans are no longer naturally aged. The best Javas nowadays are heavy bodied, with low acidity and a spicy aroma. Mellow Java still makes a fine blend with strong, bittersweet Mocha, but because the latter is so hard to find, authentic examples of the blend are very rare. A good substitute in the blend is Ethiopian Harrar. Note that the mere name Java, however, is no longer a guarantee that you are getting an *arabica* coffee, since the lower elevations have been replanted with *robusta* and *liberica* beans. Java ***

Kenya. When professional coffee traders around the world take a coffee break, they often drink a beverage made with *arabica* beans from Kenya. Kenya's coffees have the taste qualities that are available separately in other varieties from Ethiopia, Yemen, and Colombia. The beverage is full-bodied, mildly acid, a bit winey, and very smooth. Most of the Kenyan coffee crop goes to European dealers, who pay the top price for good-quality coffee, but a small share is available for Americans who are particular about their coffee flavor and aroma. Kenya AA is the top grade of Kenyan coffee and, when available, is generally a superb choice, a better buy even than the highly touted Jamaica Blue Mountain or Hawaiian Kona coffees. In Britain, Kenyan coffee is sometimes called Chagga, after the tribe that, grows it on the slopes of Mt. Kilimanjaro. Kenya AA ******

Kona. See Hawaii.

Mandheling. See Sumatra.

Maragogipe. A generic name for coffee produced from any tree that is descended from a botanical mutation of *arabica* that was discovered many years ago near the Brazilian town of Maragogipe in the state of Bahia. Although still grown in Brazil, Maragogipe trees have been planted in coffee-producing countries throughout the world. Because the Maragogipe plant tolerates the tropical heat of lowland plantations better than other *arabica* varieties, it is commonly the tree of choice for such areas. About the only thing

● ●

you can be sure of when buying a coffee identified as Maragogipe is that the bean will be huge. Generally, the bean's flavor will be determined by where it is grown. Their large size makes them popular in Europe, where they are often displayed in a cafe's glass-walled grinder. Maragogipe **—*****

Mexico. Nearly one million acres of coffee trees are grown in Mexico, on farms located in a region that extends from Hidalgo in the north to the Guatemalan border. Mexican coffees generally are full-bodied, rich, and mildly acid, with a fragrant bouquet. The better grades of Mexican coffees are the altura, or high-grown, beans produced at elevations above 1,200 meters (4,000 feet). The better Mexican coffees include Coatepec, Cordoba, Jalapa, Oaxaca, Pluma Oaxaca, and Tapachulas. Mexican coffees, especially the tangy Coatepecs, make an excellent dark roast. They also blend well with a coffee like Brazil's Bourbon Santos.

Pluma coffee was developed from Mocha seed plants. It is favored for its excellent flavor and sharp acidity, which make it suitable both as an unblended coffee and as a component in blends with East African *arabica* beans. Plumas were originally produced in the Oaxaca District but recently have been grown in other areas of Mexico, particularly the Hidalgo region. Mexico *****

Mocha. See Yemen.

Mysore. See India.

New Guinea. This coffee is grown in Papua New Guinea, the eastern side of an island shared with Indonesia. New Guinea coffee is produced on small farms and plantations and is similar in quality to other coffees from the neighboring areas of Java, Celebes (Sulawesi), and Timor. New Guinea coffee can be rich in flavor but usually is light-bodied and less aromatic than Java coffee from *arabica* beans. New Guinea ***

Peaberry. Peaberry beans, like maragogipes, are mutations of ordinary *arabica* beans. Called *caracol* in Spanish, they occur when an *arabica* cherry develops only one round bean instead of the usual two hemispherical ones. Size and shape make the peaberry attractive to those who display unground beans, but flavor depends on where the bean was grown. A Jamaican High Mountain peaberry is likely to make an exquisite coffee, whereas a Brazilian peaberry may be far from startling. Peaberry **—*****

Peru. Peruvian coffee production is rapidly expanding, especially in the Andean foothills bordering the Chanchamayo valley. The best are slightly acidy and quite flavorful, despite a rather thin body. A dark roast brings out the best in Peruvian beans. Peru *** Peru, dark-roasted ****

Rwanda. Like its neighbor Burundi, Rwanda produces only washed *arabica* coffees, most of which are exported to the United States. The very best, however, are bought by European dealers. Rwandan *arabica* coffees are highly acid, producing a rich, dark brew. Rwanda ***

Sumatra. Though the *arabica* coffees produced on this Indonesian island are scarce, they are superior to those produced on neighboring Java. Part of the reason is that Sumatra's *arabica* crop is still hand-tended and hand-picked. In general, they are rich, mellow, and relatively low in acid. Their heavy body makes them a good choice if you like your coffee with milk, since the flavor survives the mixture.

The coffee called Mandheling is the best and heaviest of all. It is so rich that, even when light-roasted, it tastes almost like an espresso roast. Almost syrupy on the palate, Mandheling also has a pro-

Site of the Merchant's Coffeehouse in New York.

nounced and pleasant aroma. Another coffee, Ankola, is not quite so rich, but still excellent. Sumatran *arabica* coffees are an excellent value. Mandheling ****** Ankola *****

Tanzania. Winey, acidy, rich, and mellow, the *arabica* coffees of Tanzania are in no way inferior to those of neighboring Kenya. The two finest are called Kilimanjaro and Plantation Bukoba. Be aware, however, that *robusta* beans are also produced in the Bukoba district, so be certain you are buying the *arabica*. The Kilimanjaro type may also be called Kibo Chagga, named after the same tribe that raises similar coffees on the Kenya side of the mountain. A rare treat is Tanzanian peaberry coffee: the mutant beans are separated out in harvesting, but they are very scarce. Drink all Tanzanian coffees straight and black. Blending or mixing such fine coffee is like putting steak sauce on chateaubriand. Kilimanjaro ****** Plantation Bukoba ****** Peaberry ******

Timor. A good-quality coffee bean is grown on the island of Timor, at the southeast end of the string of Sunda Islands that extends between Malaysia and Australia. The annual crop is small but the product is comparable to the good *arabica* beans of Java and Sumatra: heavy-bodied, mildly acid, with good flavor and aroma. Timor ****

Uganda. Since Idi Amin, Uganda has exported very little coffee. Previously known for its second-rate *robusta* beans, the country is also responsible for one fine *arabica*, Bugisu. Bugisu *****

Venezuela. The best of Venezuela's coffees grow against the Colombian border in the Andes mountains, and are shipped from the port of Maracaibo. Indeed, the beans called Cúcutas are actually grown on the Colombian side and only shipped from Venezuela. Cucutas and Táchiras taste much like Colombian beans, being rich and somewhat acidy. Táchiras are often so sharp that they are favored as the strong partner in blends. Coffee from Mérida, on the other hand, is very low in acid but not at all dull. Its delicate body is highly prized.

Another growing region surrounds the city of Caracas. Its beans make a light-bodied but pleasant brew that is very popular in Europe. Cúcuta ***** Táchira ***** Mérida ****** Caracas ****

Yemen. One of the world's classic coffees, Mocha comes only from Yemen—or the Yemens, since now there are two. The bean is named for the port from which it was shipped until a sandbar closed the harbor in the early nineteenth century. Although the bean is irregular and ugly, it produces a unique brew: piquant, bittersweet,

The finest coffee is plucked by hand.

and very full-bodied. Its high acidity makes it an excellent coffee to blend with the mellow Sumatra, Java, or milder Latin American coffees. The British like it blended with Mysore.

Grown on irrigated hillsides in the hot, dry climate of Araby, the Mocha beans are the descendants of those that sustained the dervish Omar and delighted the goatherd Kaldi. The two chief varieties of Mocha are called Hodeida Shortberry and Sanaa Mocha. Since the beans are irregular, it pays to buy those that have been graded for as much uniformity as possible. Shortberries are uniformly small beans. The grades called Mocha Extra and Mocha 1 should include beans of uniform size with a minimum of imperfections. True Mocha beans of any grade have been quite scarce since the Yemeni civil war split the country.

The confusion that has led people to identify the taste of Mocha with chocolate has its origin in the court of Louis XVI. A confection created for the king contained both chocolate and Mocha coffee, but the pastry was dubbed Mocha. Cafés and instant-coffee manufacturers continued the confusion by serving drinks containing both coffee and chocolate and calling them Mocha. The true Mocha coffee, however, has nothing to do with chocolate. Mocha ******

Zaire. Zaire grows mainly *robusta* beans, but the *arabica* beans grown in the Kivu and Ituri districts are excellent: sharply acid and full-bodied. They are fine as the strong partner in a blend. Kivus are more often seen in Europe and the United States than are Ituris. Zaire ****

BLENDED COFFEES

Breakfast. This is usually a mixture of approximately equal portions of Brazilian Santos and an African *arabica* coffee such as Tanzanian peaberry or an Ethiopian Harrar. The blend may also include a third type of *arabica*, such as a Colombian Bogota or Armenia.

House Blend. Most specialty stores offer a House Blend or Special Blend that may contain a balanced blend of a number of mild and not-so-mild coffees. The blends generally contain beans from Africa, Brazil, Colombia, Mexico, Central America, and Indonesia. The operator of the store may, if requested, explain the exact composition of his House Blend. Some blends contain only four kinds of coffee, others contain 14, so obviously there is no standard House Blend. Ask your dealer what it contains. The best advice, if you are tempted to try one, is to purchase the smallest amount to determine whether you like it.

Mocha Java. Almost every coffee store will sell a Mocha and Java blend, even though there probably is not enough true *arabica* Java and Mocha produced in a typical year to make a single cup of Mocha Java beverage for all the coffee drinkers in a major city. At one time, when the world was younger and Mocha and Java were the major sources of *arabica* coffees, the two types evolved naturally into a popular blend. Today's Mocha is likely to be a Mocha-style bean from Africa and a Java-style bean from the Malay Archipelago, which still can be a worthwhile combination of coffees.

The traditional Mocha Java blend brings together a winey, acidy Mocha and a sweetish, heavy-bodied Java, which are complementary in their effects on the palate. Other, less traditional blends, such as a combination of Kenya and Maracaibo coffees, contribute similar complementary taste effects. The best way to try this coffee blend is to buy fresh Java *arabica* beans and fresh Mocha beans and blend them yourself in a ratio of two parts Java to one part Mocha.

Neopolitan. A mixture of a Brazilian Santos bean and an African *arabica*, such as an Ethiopian Harrar, finished in a heavy, dark Italian roast and ground to a drip or espresso grind of fineness.

New Orleans. A blend of sour Brazilian beans and chicory, the latter accounting for from 20 to 40 percent of the blend. The coffee portion of the blend tends to have a harsh characteristic that coffee tasters identify as rioy, a trait of some Brazilian beans shipped from the port of Rio de Janeiro.

Roma. A blend of finely ground, dark-roasted beans, usually consisting of a New Orleans-style French roast together with a darker, Italian or espresso, roast. It usually includes beans that originated in Colombia and East Africa.

Viennese. A combination of Maracaibo and Mexican coffees finished in a variety of roasts. The Maracaibo beans may have a slightly dark roast and the Mexican beans a darker, French roast, with the blend typically consisting of one-third dark-roasted to two-thirds medium-roasted beans.

• •

INSTANT COFFEE

The mother of instant coffee was Japanese tea. Coffee processors since the 1860s had been attempting to prepare a powdered coffee extract but had produced only thick, liquid extracts or solid cakes. But in 1899, a Japanese chemist named Dr. Sartori Kato traveled to the United States to promote a powdered tea he had invented. Americans were not interested in powdered tea, but in Chicago, Dr. Kato became acquainted with local chemists and coffee roasters who encouraged him to try his tea process on coffee beans. It was a success. A Kato Coffee Company was organized and the first instant coffee was offered to the public at the Pan-American Exposition in Buffalo, New York, in 1901.

At about the same time, a Belgian-born Englishman named G. Washington was living in Guatemala City, the capital of Guatemala. Each afternoon, he was served coffee from a silver pot on a table in his orange grove. One day he noticed a brown powder that accumulated beneath the spout of the pot and tasted it. The powder was an instant coffee produced by nature in the mile-high mountain climate of Guatemala. From this phenomenon was born the G. Washington Coffee Refining Company, which dominated the instant-coffee market from about 1910 until shortly before the start of World War II.

Instant coffees are generally made by one of two commercial methods, spray drying or freeze drying. Whichever method is used, the process begins with percolation. Instant coffees are basically the beverage residue of a commercial manufacturer's huge pot of coffee.

The coffee extract that leaves the commercial percolator may resemble your homemade beverage only in name and color. Whereas you might expect to get, perhaps, 50 cups of coffee beverage per pound of ground roasted beans, a commercial percolator will squeeze the equivalent of 100 cups per pound from the coffee grounds. These pressure-cooker conditions alter the cellulose and starch molecules of the beans, changing the aroma and flavor of the brew. And the beans selected for instant coffee processing are frequently the lower-priced varieties, partly because the commercial roaster can make a product from the cheap beans that compares in flavor with a fine-grade roasted bean treated in the same manner.

The drying stage of instant-coffee manufacture drives off the natural aromas and flavors that are volatile, but similar aromas and flavors produced from the beans during percolation, hydrolysis, and extraction remain.

Many experts agree that freeze-drying causes less of a loss of natural coffee qualities than spray drying. The basic freeze-drying method consists of freezing the coffee extract that is delivered from the percolators, removing the moisture with a vacuum pump. Removing the moisture from frozen coffee extract is sometimes called *subliming*.

Commercial processers, aware that these processes may affect aroma and flavor, put a good deal of effort into *aromatizing* instant coffees. This means adding flavors back into instants to make them taste like the real thing. Coffee flavors can be fortified or modified by such techniques as adding natural coffee oils to instant powders or granules, or pumping coffee-aroma gas through the powder. The latter procedure is like the used-car dealer's technique of spraying the interior of an auto with "new car" aroma.

However your instant coffee is made, be aware that it is probably made out of *robusta* and/or poorer *arabica* beans. The Mexican saying "Nescafe no es cafe" (Nescafe isn't coffee) may be an exaggeration, but don't expect fresh coffee flavor.

HOW MUCH CAFFEINE IN COFFEE

As a general rule, tea leaves contain about twice as much caffeine as do coffee grounds. But it takes three or four times more coffee than tea, by dry weight, to make a palatable cup of beverage. As a result, a cup of tea usually contains significantly less caffeine than coffee, although the strength of either beverage can be varied by varying the amount of coffee or tea used. For the curious or caffeine-sensitive individual, however, the average caffeine content of various types of coffee are shown in the list below. (A chart for tea appears on page 97).

Coffee Variety	% Caffeine Content
Ethiopian Mocca	1.13
Santos	1.13
Minas	1.15
Santos Extra Prime	1.17
Mexico	1.17
Peru	1.20
Mexico Maragogipe	1.22
Costa Rica	1.22
Kivu *arabica*	1.25
Nicaragua Matagalpa	1.27
Cameroon *arabica*	1.27
Bugisu	1.27
Guatemala	1.32
Salvador	1.32
Java *arabica*	1.32
Venezuela	1.35
Rwanda/Burundi	1.35
Colombia	1.37
Cuba	1.37
Indian Malabar	1.37
Haiti	1.42
Robusta Congo	2.30
Robusta Uganda	2.30

DECAFFEINATED COFFEE

The very first decaffeinated coffee probably resulted from an accident in which a coffee shipment bound for Germany around 1900 was soaked by sea water coming in an open hatch. During experiments meant to rid the coffee beans of salt, it was found that subjecting them to pressurized steam forced out caffeine. German chemist Ludwig Roselius pursued the experiments further, discovering that solvents such as chloroform and benzene could also remove caffeine from coffee beans and tea leaves.

Two basic processes are used to extract caffeine from green coffee beans: the solvent method and the water method. The solvent method is a variation of the technique developed by Roselius. Instead of benzene or chloroform—or even trichloroethylene, found in the 1970s to produce cancer in laboratory animals—the solvent currently used is methylene chloride. To extract the caffeine, coffee beans are placed in a rotating drum and exposed to steam and methylene chloride for 12 to 18 hours. Then the beans are treated with live steam to flush out the caffeine-bearing solvent. The beans are then ready to be dried and roasted.

Though no decaffeinated bean will yield the same flavor as its undecaffeinated counterpart, gourmets who must reduce their caffeine intake prefer to drink coffee that has been decaffeinated by the water process. Solvent is still used in this process, but the solvent never touches the bean itself. Instead, the raw beans are soaked in hot water, which leaches both oils and caffeine out of them. The solution is then removed to another chamber, where the solvent is added. The solvent combines with the caffeine and is separated out, leaving the purified solution. This solution is then put back into the chamber containing the beans, where the beans reabsorb the oils. These procedures are still not completely effective at removing traces of solvent from the final product, but many drinkers think a better-tasting coffee is the result. Swiss and German companies developed the water process and are its main practitioners. For added cachet, some stores label their decaffeinated beans as Swiss Water Decaffeinated, but the important thing to note is that the water process was used.

Literally hundreds of variations of the two basic methods have been patented in the twentieth century. Most attempt to remove about 97 percent of the initial caffeine content from the green coffee beans by repeating the process up to 15 times, each removing a smaller percentage of the original caffeine content.

In shopping for decaffeinated coffees, remember that *robusta* beans generally contain twice as much caffeine as *arabica* beans. A decaffeinated *robusta*, therefore, would still contain twice as much caffeine as a decaffeinated *arabica* after 97 percent of the caffeine has been removed. And all decaffeinated coffees are not processed to remove 97 percent of the caffeine. Therefore, all decaffeinated coffees are not equally caffeine-free.

4.
Making Coffee

Brewing coffee is a simple art—smash the roasted beans, force hot water through the particles, and serve the resulting infusion piping hot. Notwithstanding the simplicity of the process, generations of coffee lovers have created any number of ways of accomplishing it. This section includes descriptions of all the devices used for grinding and brewing coffee, with comments on the advantages of each. However, there are a few general rules to follow, whatever process you use.

Some like their coffee strong, and some like it weak. The more ground coffee you use per cup of water, the stronger the drink will taste. A good benchmark measure is about 10 grams—one rounded tablespoon—of ground coffee for each 6-ounce cup. The coffee measures often included in cans of coffee or supplied with new grinders hold about this amount of coffee. At this ratio, 1 pound of coffee beans will yield about 45 cups of coffee. Some people add one extra measure "for the pot". Doing so makes the brew a bit stronger, but if the beans are fresh the extra spoonful should not be necessary.

Another factor in making coffee is the length of time it is brewed. Some people believe that they can stretch a pound of coffee by using less and brewing it longer. Unfortunately, extended brewing will extract not only the flavorful oils of the coffee but also certain bitter, astringent substances. Over-brewed coffee tastes bad. Users of percolators should take special care. Coffee should percolate for 6 to 8 minutes, but no more. Drip coffee needs only 4 to 6 minutes; vacuum and espresso coffees need only 1 to 3 minutes.

However you make your coffee, serve it as soon as it is ready. Flavor changes noticeably within less than an hour after brewing. Indeed, one of the reasons for the success of the espresso method in public cafes is that it permits the server to brew each customer a fresh cup of coffee. Many workaday coffee drinkers have had the unpleasant experience of drinking restaurant coffee, apparently brewed in the Pleistocene era, that had a flavor like nothing so much as soaked pencil leads.

GRINDING

Properly grinding the roasted bean enhances the flavor of coffee, but ground coffee also loses its flavor quickly. While the finer grinds of coffee increase the number of bean-particle surfaces exposed to the hot water in the coffee brewer, they also expose more of the particle surfaces to the oxygen in the air. Oxygen combines with the aromatic chemicals in the bean to promote staleness. Once it has been ground, the coffee should be used as rapidly as possible.

Grinding your own beans, therefore, is not a mere affectation. Coffee beans that have not been ground will retain their flavor from two to three times as long as ground beans. Although the flavor of the bean is established in the roasting process, the substances that are responsible for the flavor are locked inside the bean until it is pulverized in a grinder. The locked-in flavor of whole, roasted beans can be extended by grinding only as many beans as you need for each batch of beverage.

A freshly roasted bean will hold its flavor at room temperature for about a week, so unless you live a long way from a reliable supplier or want to store a quantity in the freezer, buy only the amount of whole roasted beans you expect to use in a week. A pound of coffee is usually enough for six or eight cups a day for a week.

If you make your own blends, be wary of accumulating a large variety of different kinds of coffee. They can become stale faster than you can savor the results of your experiments. If you have a friend who also enjoys blending and brewing coffees from the original beans, you can share purchases or trade the excess quantities.

Coffee grinders are not all alike. In stores that handle merchandise from the Middle East, it is possible to purchase a heavy brass mortar and pestle of the type that has been used in the Levant for centuries to grind coffee beans. This method substitutes human muscle power for electric power but it is effective and is guaranteed to strengthen the wrists and arms. Since it has no moving parts of its own, the mortar and pestle set can last a lifetime with no repairs. The French gourmet Brillat-Savarin opined that coffee powdered in a pestle made a better brew than beans that were ground. The method, however, is labor-intensive.

A more convenient hand-operated grinder is the box-type mill. A box coffee mill is a small wooden box with a metal hopper in the top and a crank handle in the middle of the hopper. Turning the crank moves a set of gears inside the box that grind the beans as they drop through the funnel-shaped hopper. A drawer at the bottom of the box collects the ground coffee. This kind of grinder has been in use in Europe and North America since the nineteenth century. Until the 1930s, the box mill was a regular item in most American department stores, but today they are most easily found in such specialty stores as gourmet food shops, import shops, or antique shops. By carefully browsing in antique

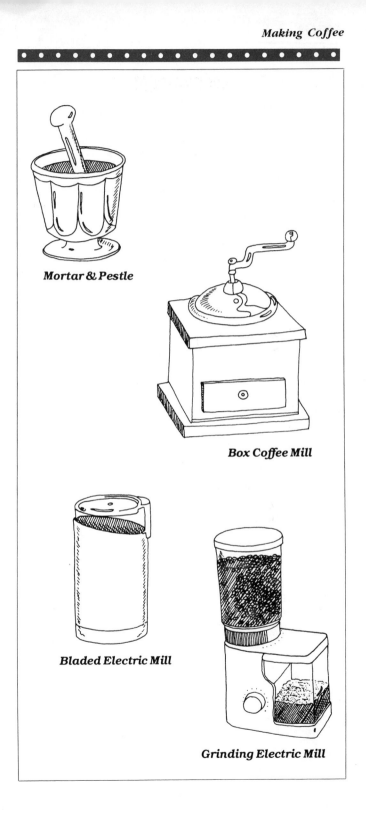

Mortar & Pestle

Box Coffee Mill

Bladed Electric Mill

Grinding Electric Mill

· ·

HOW FINE TO GRIND

Method	Grind
Turkish	powdered
Filter	very fine
Espresso	fine
Drip	fine
Vacuum	fine
Percolator	medium
Steeped	medium

stores, you may find an old hand-operated coffee grinder from the pre-1930 era at a price that is no more than the cost of a 1980s model imported from the Orient.

Some users of the box coffee mill are not satisfied with its limited control over grinds—a complaint that may be justified since the device was designed originally for the typical rural home of a century ago when commercially ground and vacuum-packed cans of coffee were unheard of. However, all the models have wing nuts or regulator nuts that can be turned clockwise or counterclockwise for finer or coarser grinds of coffee. If you brew coffee in a percolator, a box mill will do fine, but if you use a drip or espresso machine, opt for an electric grinder.

A variation of the box coffee mill is the wall-mounted grinder which requires two hands to operate: one to hold the box under the grinder and one to turn the crank. It is premounted on a square of wood that is attached to a wall or side of a cabinet with four wood screws. Like the box coffee mill, the wall- or side-mounted mill, is operated by turning a crank on a shaft after beans are poured into the hopper. It also has a screw that permits rough control over the size of the grind.

Miniature versions of the old-fashioned grocery-store coffee grinder, featuring a big wheel on either side and a handle on one wheel to drive the grinder, also are available in the same price range as some of the box or side-mill grinders. All the hand-powered grinders do require some physical effort, but it is hardly strenuous. In fact, the notion seems to appeal to individuals who seek ways of getting back to the basic work methods. And the devices do contribute a bit of old-fashioned decor to the kitchen area.

Electric coffee grinders, or mills (the terms are often used interchangeably by manufacturers and salespeople), are available in two types: one has a set of whirling blades at the bottom of a bean hopper, similar to the blades found in some electric food blenders; the other is like an electrical version of the old hand-operated grinders, with burr-shaped discs that crush the beans into particles. Higher prices are charged for the kind that grind rather than slice the beans into tiny pieces.

Most electric mills can produce grinds suitable for all but Turkish-style preparations. The bladed mills ordinarily produce a moderately fine grind comparable to a commercial drip grind. A finer grind can be obtained by running the mill for a longer time. True grinders, which mangle the bean between revolving burrs, usually can be set for a range of grinds. Both kinds of mill can produce good ground coffee, but the true grinder has one advantage. The bladed mill slices the beans into long, flat-faceted fragments, while the burr-ground coffee presents more surfaces to the hot water, so it brews faster and stronger. The difference may be scarcely perceptible to the average coffee drinker, but perfectionists will insist on true grinding. If you want your coffee ground as fine as wheat flour, you will have to resort to the mortar and pestle.

BREWING

IBRIK

The earliest bona fide coffee maker was the *ibrik*, the small brass pot with a long narrow handle that is still used in Middle Eastern restaurants that serve Turkish or Armenian coffee. It is a very simple device, containing two or three cups of water and held over the fire until the water boils. It is then removed, the finely ground coffee is put directly into the water, and it is brought once again to a boil. In fact, it may be boiled and allowed to cool briefly several times before it is served.

The *ibrik* makes a very thick coffee. Sugar may be added to the beverage. And, as is done by many coffee consumers of the Levant, the wet, pulverized, and sweetened coffee grounds can be ingested along with the liquid portion of the beverage. When coffee was introduced to Europeans in the seventeenth century, much of it was prepared in and served from *ibriks*, and the small, demitasse-size cups or glasses of the Middle East were the vessels from which the first European coffee imbibers took the beverage in "little swallows."

By the start of the eighteenth century, Europeans had begun designing larger and fancier coffee pots made of gold, silver, tin, or porcelain. They had lids and handles at right angles to the pouring spouts, but the coffee was still boiled. The break-through to modern methods of coffee-making occurred in France in 1802, when a patent was granted for a "pharmacological-chemical coffee-making device by infusion." At about the same time, coffee makers in the form of distillation contrivances, drip pots, and percolators began to appear throughout North America and Europe.

Except for the *ibrik* users of the world and some die-hard outdoor types, few people today boil their coffee. Most homes use either a drip coffee maker or a percolator. And the modern percolator is sometimes identified as a pump percolator, because it contains a pump tube through which the hot water is forced up and over the ground coffee by the pressure of the steam vapor bubbles that form around the source of heat at the bottom.

● ●

DRIP

The modern drip coffee maker receives the hot water from a reservoir or container above the grounds. The water drips through the ground coffee and into a carafe below. Some coffee lovers claim that drip coffee is superior because the hot water passes through the ground coffee only once. (Percolator enthusiasts prefer a beverage made by having the hot water recirculated through the ground coffee). In a blind test conducted a few years ago by the Consumers Union, only a coffee expert was able to determine whether a cup of coffee had been made by the drip or the percolator method.

The automatic drip coffee maker is similar to the traditional drip coffee maker except that it has a reservoir of hot water that is released into the coffee grounds when fresh tap or bottled water is added to the reservoir. The automatic drip coffee maker also uses a paper filter liner for the basket holding the coffee grounds. After the hot coffee has finished dripping through the filter, the basket can be turned upside-down over an open trash bag. The filter with wet grounds drops out and, after being rinsed in warm water, the basket is ready for another batch of coffee.

● ●

VACUUM

The vacuum coffee maker is a complicated device in which steam is generated in a glass bowl connected to a holding container of coffee grounds and hot water. When the heat under the glass bowl is removed, the reduced pressure causes a partial vacuum that draws the hot water through the coffee grounds and into the glass bowl.

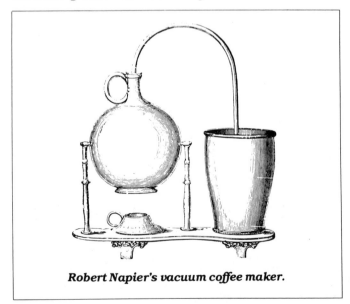

Robert Napier's vacuum coffee maker.

The vacuum coffee maker was invented in 1840 by the Scottish scientist Robert Napier, who failed to obtain a patent for the device. However, many variations of the original vacuum coffee maker appeared on the market in subsequent years, each patented by an individual who claimed to have found a way to improve on the Napier invention. One required a hand pump to help force the hot water through the coffee grounds, which were contained in a perforated chamber that had to be screwed to the bottom of the coffee maker. Few coffee drinkers today would have the time or inclination to follow the steps required to obtain coffee by such a laborious method.

With the development of heat-resistant glass, vacuum coffee makers enjoyed a long period of popularity, particularly in the United States during the twenties and thirties, because the design enables a person to watch a dramatic beverage-making process. The vacuum is still quite popular in Japan, especially in the finer Koohi Shoppus (coffee shops).

PERCOLATOR

A half-century ago, nearly three-fourths of the homes in North America prepared coffee in a pump percolator, especially an electric model with the heat element built into the bottom of the pot. Although many coffee lovers still swear by the electric percolator, all electric percolators do not make a good cup of coffee and do not make a cup of coffee quickly. Because a pump percolator usually has a glass top through which one can see the hot water spurting, an illusion is created that the water is boiling hot. But it is the pumping action that causes the fountain spray of water at the top, not the temperature of the water. As a result, an electric percolator often fails to do a proper job of extracting coffee from the grounds. Furthermore, a stove-top pump percolator can produce coffee in less than 10 minutes, but some electric percolators require more than 20 minutes to yield a questionable tepid beverage.

PLUNGER

A type of coffee maker preferred by some is the European plunger, which consists of a glass cylinder with a metal rod extending through the center. Protruding from the top end of the rod is a plastic knob, and at the bottom end is a perforated plunger that fits snugly around the inside of the glass cylinder. Coffee grounds are placed in the cylinder and boiling hot water is poured over the grounds. They are allowed to steep, like tea, for about five minutes. Then the plunger is pushed down over the wet grounds to separate the beverage from the grounds. The hot coffee is then poured from the glass cylinder. The beverage is strong and bitter, a brew that appeals to some coffee drinkers.

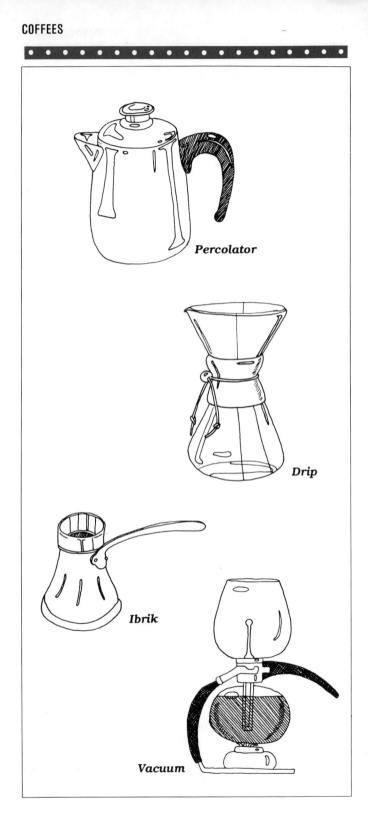

Percolator

Drip

Ibrik

Vacuum

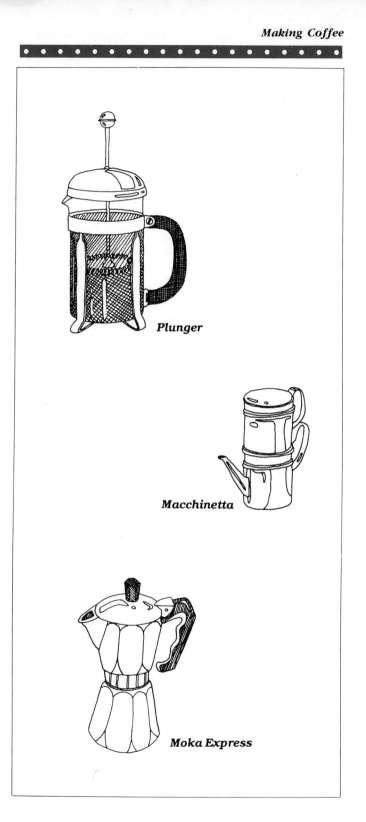

Plunger

Macchinetta

Moka Express

- -

MACCHINETTA

A macchinetta consists of two metal cylinders, one with a pouring spout, and a small coffee basket that fits between the two cylinders. Water is poured into the cylinder without the spout, two level tablespoons of drip- or fine-ground Italian-roast coffee are placed in the basket for each demitasse-sized cup of beverage desired, the parts are fitted together carefully, and the complete device is placed over the flame. When steam begins to shoot from a tiny hole in the lower part of the macchinetta, the whole brewer is removed from the heat and turned upside down. The boiling water filters through the coffee grounds into the cylinder with the spout and the beverage is ready to serve. Coffee from a macchinetta is a delightful brew, even though it is not really espresso. For the purist, macchinetta coffee is called Italian coffee. It may even be spelled on the menus in the Italian way with two f's and one e, as in *caffé*.

- -

ESPRESSO

The term espresso is derived from the Italian word for speed. Many Americans call it expresso. But the meaning has been lost in the years since espresso was introduced, and today the word suggests a small cup of hot, dark coffee that is consumed at a leisurely pace rather than in a hurry. It is not the coffee-break drink or the coffee for a last sip before rushing off to the job. Espresso is the coffee to have at the end of a good meal, when there is time to relax and linger.

Technically, espresso coffee is a beverage made in an espresso machine, a device designed to brew coffee instantaneously under steam pressure. There are a number of different kinds of espresso machines on the market. There are also coffee makers that sometimes pass for espresso devices but that are actually small Italian-style drip pots called *macchinetta* (see above).

The original espresso machines were invented in 1903, more or less simultaneously in Milan and Turin. Desiderio Pavoni, in Milan, built his machine to produce 150 cups of coffee an hour with steam pressure. He called his machine Ideale. In Turin, meanwhile, Pier Teresio Arduino designed an espresso machine that would turn out 1,000 individual cups of coffee an hour. Arduino named his machine for his wife, La Victoria Arduino. Arduino also introduced the tradition of decorating the espresso machine with a picture of an eagle or condor. The machine was a towering boiler with spigots, handles, and gauges. Each spigot was designed to hold a filter containing enough strong, finely ground, dark-roasted coffee for one cup of espresso. Turning the spigot allowed a shot of steaming hot water to be forced through the coffee grounds, producing an instant cup of real coffee. However, the original espresso machines did have their shortcomings. Too much hot steam could scald the coffee grounds, yielding a cup of bitter, overly extracted coffee.

SERVING ESPRESSO

Espresso should be served with a twist of lemon peel or a thin slice of lemon. Espresso with a bit of lemon flavor is sometimes identified as Roman-style espresso, or espresso Romano. For those who like exotic variations, a bit of spice or extract, such as a touch of cardamom or a genuine vanilla bean for stirring, might enhance the serving. Sugar is permitted but cream is never added to a smooth, full-bodied cup of espresso.

For those who like an espresso brew with milk, the Italians invented cappuccino, a word derived from the name of the Capuchin order of Franciscan monks. Properly prepared with steaming milk and steaming coffee, a cup of caffè cappuccino can satisfy the palates of any who insist that straight espresso coffee is too sharp or bitter.

Caffè cappuccino requires hot espresso and hot—but not boiling—foaming milk. Milk that is not steaming hot will cool the espresso to insipid tepidness. An espresso machine equipped with cappuccino accessories makes this step relatively easy, since there should be a valve that allows a jet of steam to rush into the cold milk, foaming it while heating it. It will take some practice to adjust the jet of steam so it heats and foams the milk properly without boiling it. If you don't have facilities for producing foaming milk with jets of steam, just heat the milk—be sure not to boil it.

When using foamed milk, first fill one-third of the cup with hot milk; next add one-third cup of hot espresso; one-third cup of milk foam goes on the top. When ordinary hot milk is used with espresso, a half-and-half mixture works quite well, but still it's best to put the milk into the cup before the espresso.

Caffè cappuccino, like plain espresso, can be served with sugar. Add a bit of gastronomic versatility with a sprinkling of nutmeg, cinnamon, or other appropriate spices, or a combination of spices and extracts. Nutmeg and cinnamon usually contribute complementary flavors.

Chocolate also goes well with espresso or cappuccino. One favorite of espresso lovers is Caffè Borgia, prepared by combining equal quantities of espresso or macchinetta coffee and hot chocolate. The mixture is topped with sweetened whipped cream and a sprinkling of grated orange peel. Another chocolate variation is a tall cup of cappuccino topped with whipped cream and a mound of shavings of French chocolate. The name? Caffè Chocolaccino.

Iced espresso is a pleasant warm-weather drink. Fill a six-ounce glass, or cup, with cracked ice and pour in a demitasse-size serving of hot espresso. Then add a small amount of simple sugar syrup and a long curl of lemon peel, and serve. The sugar syrup can be made in advance by mixing equal amounts of sugar and water in a saucepan. Simmer the mixture for about five minutes, or until the sugar is completely dissolved. Then remove the mixture and pour it into a covered jar and store it in the refrigerator. It keeps indefinitely and is handy to have around for easy sweetening of coffee and tea beverages.

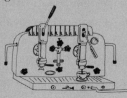

New and better designs of espresso machines appeared after World War II. A horizontal boiler was introduced that prevented scalding. The resulting brew was so smooth and flavorful that it was promoted briefly as cream coffee. Customers continued to call the product espresso as before.

Few homes can afford the space and expense required for a commercial espresso machine, but there are a number of small machines on the market that very closely reproduce the quality produced by the larger devices. The principle of operation is essentially the same: steaming hot water is forced through finely ground, dark-roasted coffee so that the maximum extraction of the coffee liquor is achieved in the minimum amount of time.

Satisfactory home espresso coffee makers are sold in a number of department and specialty stores at prices ranging over a wide scale. Not unexpectedly, the more expensive versions make a smoother cup of espresso and usually come with accessories for preparing cappuccino as well. They depend either on a hand-pulled lever whose spring action forces hot water through the ground coffee, or on hydraulic pressure that requires only the energy needed to push a button to start the process. A typical hydraulic-powered espresso machine contains a hot-water reservoir that holds enough water for 20 servings and an electric element to control the temperature of the water.

Less elaborate but almost as effective are the stove-top espresso pots, the original model of which was called Moka Express. In these machines, the water vapor that is created just before boiling is forced through the coffee grounds and into an upper reservoir, where it condenses back into liquid and from which it can be served. The Moka Express and its imitators make a fine cup of espresso, but you should look for the models made of stainless steel rather than aluminum. The latter leaves an unpleasant taste in the coffee.

Remember when planning your espresso needs that espresso is usually measured in demitasse sizes. For a regular cup of coffee or tea, double everything. When purchasing the equipment, don't be misled by the number of cups claimed by the promotional material to be the machine's capacity, because the yield in full cups is often less. It's better to select an espresso maker that may be too large than to invest in one that may not be adequate.

● ●

TURKISH COFFEE RITUAL

Although Turkey is not a coffee-producing country, Turkish coffee is almost as famous as Mocha and Java. One reason is that the Turks probably have contributed more to the mystique of coffee-drinking than any other of the world's cultures. The traditional Turkish coffee ceremony is still practiced in many parts of the world, where Middle Eastern people gather for social or business purposes. Even when you order Turkish coffee in an authentic Middle Eastern restaurant, you are served more than a demitasse cup of a sweet, thick, strong coffee. You are provided a small share of an ancient tradition symbolizing the finest of Middle Eastern hospitality.

Good Turkish coffee should have foam or froth on the surface when it is served, in accordance with a cardinal rule of the Turkish coffee ceremony which states that "if the froth is absent from the face of the coffee, the host loses face." The froth is produced by bringing the coffee to a boil three times without allowing it to boil over. The cone-shaped pot, or *ibrik*, is ideal for the ceremony since it permits the froth from each "boil-up" to accumulate until there is enough foam for each of the cups that will share the contents of the *ibrik*.

The complete ceremony requires that the host start with a supply of green beans, one way to assure the guests that the coffee they will be served will be prepared from freshly roasted beans. The beans are dark-roasted, then ground to a fine powder using a heavy brass mortar with a brass pestle. Spices such as cardamom, cloves, or cinnamon may be mixed with the coffee as it is being ground.

Approximately 1 tablespoon of ground coffee is used for each demitasse serving of about 3 fluid ounces. During the first boil, 1 teaspoon of sugar is added to the mixture for each serving. If a spice was not mixed with the coffee during the grinding step, it usually is added during the boiling. Each time the coffee is brought to a boil, it is removed from the heat.

When the coffee has gone through its third "boil-up," it is removed from the heat and poured in the demitasse cups for serving. By tradition, the host is served first and takes a sip of the beverage to demonstrate that it contains no harmful substance. Otherwise, the guests are served according to their rank or stature. Because of the honor of being invited to participate in the ceremony, it is considered impolite to refuse to accept a cup of the coffee.

Turkish coffee is taken as hot as the mouth can tolerate. It is to be sipped slowly and gently, almost as if it were being inhaled, so that each molecule of fragrance and flavor can be appreciated. Swallowing the coffee grounds is not mandatory, but it is usual.

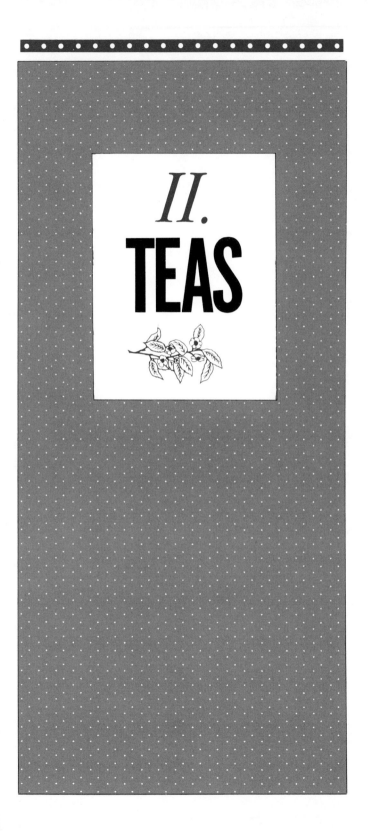

II.
TEAS

1.
Tea in History

Tea has a myriad of shapes. If I may speak vulgarly
and rashly, tea may shrink and crinkle like a Mongol's
boots. Or it may look like the dewlap of a wild ox, some
sharp, some curling as the eaves of a house. It can look like
a mushroom in whirling flight or just as clouds do when
they float out from behind a mountain peak. Its leaves can
swell and leap as if they were being lightly tossed in wind
disturbed water. Others will look like clay, soft and mal-
leable, prepared for the hand of the potter and will be as
clear and as pure as if filtered through wood. Still others
will twist and turn like rivulets carved out by violent rain
on newly tilled fields.

So Lu Yu, in his *Ch'a Ching (Tea Classic)* written in 780
A.D., expressed the passion of the Chinese for the various
manifestations of their favorite beverage. Tea has been
consumed, cultivated, and esteemed as virtually holy by the
Chinese since the fourth century. Strangely, when Marco
Polo returned to Italy in 1295 after twenty years in China, he
told of gunpowder and pasta, but never mentioned tea. It
took another three hundred years for tea to make its first
mark on the European imagination, and another hundred
more for it to evoke passions and rhetorical displays to rival
those of the *Ch'a Ching.*

The first printed reference to tea in European literature
was in a book of travelers' tales compiled in 1559 by
Giambattista Ramusio, a Venetian nobleman. One of the
travelers, a Persian merchant named Hajji Mahommed, told
Ramusio how the Chinese made use of a certain plant:

This is called by those people Chai Catai.... *They take of
that herb, whether dry or fresh, and boil it well in water.
One or two cups of this decoction taken on an empty
stomach removes fever, headache, stomach ache, pain in
the side or in the joints, and it should be taken as hot as
you can bear it. He said, besides, that it was good for no end
of other ailments which he could not remember, but gout
was one of them.... And it is so highly valued and
esteemed that every one going on a journey takes it with
him, and those people would gladly give a sack of rhubarb
for one ounce of* Chai Catai. *And those people of Cathay do*

Fired tea leaves were once sorted by hand.

say if [in] our parts of the world, in Persia, and the country of the Franks, people only knew of it, there is no doubt that the merchants would cease altogether to buy rhubarb.

Sound like an advertisement? Well, in a sense it was. Many of the travelogues of this time were written chiefly to stir up demand for oriental goods. Interestingly, until the herb became commonplace in Europe, most of the accounts of tea describe it in almost exactly the same terms as Mahommed, as if the writers copied either each other or a single Chinese source.

For centuries, silks, spices, rhubarb, and other oriental goods could only be transported overland to Europe by Persian caravans. However, in the early sixteenth century, the Portuguese and Spanish developed long-range sailing ships, which allowed them to travel to China entirely by sea. By cutting out the Persian middlemen and by transporting the goods in larger quantities, the Portuguese were able to undersell their competitors, the Venetians, thus becoming Europe's chief purveyors of oriental delicacies. As a consequence of their direct contact with the East, the Portuguese were also the first Europeans to actually sample the prized Chinese beverage called either *Ch'a* or *T'e*, depending on whether you sipped it in Canton or Amoy. Father Matteo Ricci, a missionary who spent twelve years in China, sent home copious accounts of tea, describing it as having "a peculiar mild bitterness, not disagreable to the taste."

● ● ● ● ● ● ● ● ● ● ● ● ● ● ● ● ● ● ●

Although the Portuguese and Spanish dominated oriental trade throughout most of the sixteenth century, they were dependent on Dutch gold for financial backing. The Dutch, then under Spanish rule, were also the main European distributors of the goods that Portuguese ships brought home. In 1581, Holland broke with Spain and declared itself an independent republic, and in 1588, the Spanish Armada was soundly trounced by the British Navy. These developments signalled the end for Spain and Portugal as world powers. The two nations could do little more than watch helplessly as the Dutch and the English moved in on their Eastern markets.

The Dutch moved first, inspired by yet another advertisement disguised as travelogue. In 1595, Jan Hugo van Lin-Schooten, a Dutch seaman who had served with the Portuguese, published *Discourse of Voyages*, an account of his travels that contained an eloquent description of Japanese tea-drinking habits. Within a year after the book's appearance, the Dutch established a trading post on Bantam, an island near Java. It was from this trading post that the first consignment of tea was sent to Europe in 1606.

The herb was not an overnight sensation. The first tea to reach Dutch ports was not ordered, but was sent as a kind of afterthought, whenever there was a little extra room on board ship. It wasn't until 1637 that the directors of the Dutch East India Company began to wonder if there might not be some profit in the herb and sent the following message to their agents in Bantam: "As tea begins to come into use with some people, we expect some jars of Chinese, as well as Japanese tea with each ship."

The people with whom tea came into use were largely "high princes and grandees" (as one tea merchant was later to describe them) who had both the connections and the income to purchase the novel herb. Little by little the demand for tea grew, encouraged no doubt by the efforts of people like Dr. Cornelius Decker, better known as Dr. Bontekoe (Dr. Goodtea), who described the medicinal uses of tea in his *Diatribe on Fevers:*

It must be a considerable and obstinate fever that cannot be cured by drinking every day forty to fifty cups of tea, about twenty of which are strong and bitter. This is an effect that we have proven recently on several patients and this is why we now reject all remedies we used to use to cure such sicknesses.... We recommend in particular the use of tea for all sorts of people of both sexes, young and old, for this nation and all other peoples, and we advise them to drink it every day, at all times, all hours, as much as they can drink, beginning with eight to ten cups and eventually augmenting the dose to whatever amounts the stomach can hold.

Dr. Goodtea himself claimed to drink 200 cups of tea a day, without any ill effects. It will come as no surprise, however, that he was later found to be in the employ of the Dutch East India Company. Tea won praise from plenty of other, more independent, authorities, but it was also the object of condemnation from physicians who warned that the infusion "hastened death" and would even cause Europeans to develop oriental features.

How much these warnings slowed, or perhaps accelerated, the growth of tea's popularity is not known, but by the 1680s the Dutch East India Company was demanding that thousands of pounds of tea be put on every ship. As the supply increased, the price gradually fell, and tea began to be consumed not only by the aristocracy but by the bourgeois and working classes, and not only in Holland but in Germany and France as well.

Tea also reached Europe via Russia. As early as 1567, Russian travelers returned overland from China with news of the drink. The first jars of tea were carried to Moscow in 1638, but did not make much of an impression. It wasn't until 1689, when the Tsar signed a trade agreement with China, that tea began to be regularly imported via caravan across the Siberian waste, soon becoming the rage of Moscow.

The Russians developed a style of tea-drinking unlike that of either Europe or Asia. The most important item in the Russian tea service was, and is to this day, the samovar: a large water-heating urn with a pot of very strong tea resting on top of it. A small amount of tea is poured from the pot into a glass, which is then filled with hot water from a spigot at the bottom of the samovar. A slice of lemon and a spoonful of jam are added for flavoring. The Russians often sweeten their tea not by adding sugar to the drink, but by sipping it through a lump of sugar held between the teeth.

The English, by far the world's most celebrated tea drinkers, were among the last to develop a taste for the herb. Coffee was the beverage that caught the British fancy, and coffeehouses, the first of which opened in 1650, were hotbeds of gossip, literary discussion, and subversive politicking. Most of the tea that entered England during the first half of the seventeenth century was procured by wealthy individuals while they traveled on the continent, particularly in France, where in 1648 tea was called the impertinent novelty of the age. It was the French who initiated the custom, so heartily embraced by the British, of mixing milk with tea.

However, in 1657 Thomas Garway distributed a broadside that announced that tea, formerly available only to "high princes and grandees" could now be purchased in his London coffeehouse. Since tea cost the equivalent of 30 to 50 dollars a pound, during a time when a good meal at an inn could be had for 12 cents, Garway made a point of emphasizing that "The leaf is of such known vertues, that those very Nations famous for Antiquity, Knowledge and Wisdom, do frequently sell it among themselves for twice its weight in silver." Garway's argument must have been effective because, despite the exorbitant cost, tea was soon being offered by many other coffeehouses.

The most important proponent of tea in England was the Infanta Catherine Braganza who, having grown up a tea-drinker in Portugal, was in no way disposed to give up her habit when she married Britain's king, Charles II. Tea soon replaced ale as the beverage of choice at many court occasions. On Catherine's first birthday in her new country, Edmund Waller presented her with the following poem:

Venus her Myrtle, Phoebus has her bays;
Tea both excels, which she vouchsafe to praise.
The best of Queens, and best of herbs, we owe
To that bold nation, which the way did show
To the fair regions where the sun doth rise,
Whose rich production we so justly prize.
The Muse's friend, tea doth our fancy aid,
Repress those vapours which the head invade,
And keep the palace of the soul serene,
Fit on her birthday to salute the Queen.

Waller, it should be noted, drank his tea by the pint, with a couple of egg yolks beaten into it.

While Catherine was creating a fashion for tea at court, the

A Russian family gathered around the samovar.

British East India Company finally caught on that there was a profit to be made from tea, and began importing it directly from China. The decline in price of the herb that resulted, coupled with the lure of fashion, made the coffeehouses that served tea immensely popular, but only at the expense of inns and taverns. Noting the decline in revenues from the liquor tax, Charles II levied a tax on tea, thereby somewhat mitigating the fashion his wife had inspired. One can't help but speculate about the discussions this tax sparked in the royal household.

Surprisingly, it was alcohol, not coffee, that was tea's main competitor during the seventeenth and eighteenth centuries. Tea fell out of fashion in Germany because it couldn't compete with beer, and in France because, in the words of one critic, "The best tea of the Celestial Empire cannot bear a comparison with Bordeaux, Burgundy and Champagne." Such a comparison may seem ludicrous to a modern reader, but it should be remembered that even in England men, women, and children all started the day with a pint of ale. It wasn't until 1702 that another queen, Anne, created a stir by serving tea at court breakfasts ("And thou Great Anna, whom three realms obey,/Did sometimes Council take—and sometimes tea," wrote Alexander Pope, wryly noting his queen's persuasion). And even though tea consumption rose tremendously over the next 100 years, the average gentleman in the eighteenth century still managed to drink four bottles of wine a day. Given that statistic, it's a wonder the English had any time or impulse to drink tea at all.

In 1745, the duty on tea was cut to one penny, causing the amount of tea retained for home consumption to more than triple: from 360,000 kilograms (800,000 pounds) during the years 1741–45, to over 1.2 million kilograms (2.5 million pounds) during 1746–50. During the eighteenth century, as the English became more familiar with the herb and how to brew it, they began to drink most of their tea at home. Many of the old coffeehouses (which had also served tea) closed or turned into taverns. However, even though the price of tea had fallen to between 2 and 36 shillings per pound, it was still exorbitantly expensive to the working class, who were commonly paid a shilling a week. They bought it, nonetheless, in small quantities, drinking it very weak. Or, alternatively, they bought tea cheap from smugglers who often adulterated it with sawdust or sloe leaves.

Jonas Hanway, philanthropist, pamphleteer, and popularizer of the umbrella (which some say he invented) was so alarmed by the rise in tea consumption among the lower classes that he felt compelled to append a polemic against the beverage to an article he wrote on an entirely unrelated topic. "The very chambermaids have lost their bloom by drinking tea," he declared, and went on to berate tea for being "pernicious to health, obstructing industry and impoverishing the neighborhood." Tea found itself a worthy defender in Samuel Johnson, who, in his review of Hanway's piece, declared himself a "hardened and shameless tea-drinker, who has for many years diluted his meals with only the infusion of this fascinating plant; whose kettle has scarcely had time to cool; who with tea amuses the evening, with tea solaces the midnight and with tea welcomes the morning." His biographer, Sir John Hawkins, corroborates Johnson's love for the leaf, but casts it in a slightly different light: "Whenever (tea) appeared he was almost raving, and by his impatience to be served, his incessant calls for those ingredients which make the liquor palatable, and the haste with which he swallowed it down, he seldom failed to make that a fatigue to everyone which was intended as a general refreshment."

It seems that after two hundred years tea was at last able to evoke both passions and rhetorical outbursts in Europeans that rivaled in intensity if not in nature those of Lu Yu in his *Tea Classic*.

As the origins of tea itself remain shrouded in obscurity, so do the origins of that venerable institution, teatime. Perhaps this is because among the British, as the Mad Hatter remarked to Alice, it's always teatime. In any event, some historians credit Anna, the wife of the Seventh Duke of Bedford, with starting the custom around 1840. Most historians, however, seem to think teatime evolved gradually during the eighteenth century, though there is some disagreement as to whether it was a prelude or postlude to the major meal of the day. One theory says that it was both. Among the aristocrats, "tea" was a small meal of pastries and sandwiches served with tea at about 6 P.M., to help famished lords and ladies endure until the main meal of the day, which began around 9 P.M. The bourgeois and working classes had their main meal at noon, so "tea" for them, often called "meat tea" or "high tea," consisted of leftover meat, cheese, bread, and of course tea, served as the evening meal. The aristocratic "tea," perhaps at the instigation of Anna, Duchess of Bedford, eventually came to be served at 4 P.M., and this is the hour we traditionally think of as teatime. But among some of the working class, particularly in the north of England, "tea" is still a large meal served at the end of the day.

Surprisingly, tea was more popular in North America than it was in London during much of the seventeenth century. The Dutch, who introduced tea to Europe, brought it with them when they founded New Amsterdam in 1626. Archeologists have found that the first homes in what is now New York City contained the finest Dutch teapots, teacups, tea boards, tea strainers, and spoons. The old Knickerbockers were such connoisseurs of the leaf that housewives customarily served steaming pots of different kinds of teas to their guests. The Dutch did not drink their tea with milk, but flavored it with saffron or peach leaves, and sweetened it in one of two ways: either they nibbled a lump of sugar as they sipped, or they stirred powdered sugar into their cups; hence, tea tables were provided with partitioned *bite* and *stir* boxes.

The manifest of the *Mayflower* shows a coffee grinder among the items in the cargo, but tea drinking in the English colonies apparently did not become popular until the very end of the seventeenth century. When at last they did pick up the tea habit, the early settlers of New England displayed true Puritan frugality. They boiled the herb until

every bit of flavor had been extracted, producing a dark and bitter brew. Then, when the teapot was empty, they did not throw away the leaves, but spooned them onto toast and ate them with butter and salt. They also were sparing with their crockery. Guests at tea parties customarily brought their own cups, saucers, and spoons.

When New York came under British rule, public tea gardens modeled on London's Vauxhall and Ranelagh pleasure gardens became the gathering places of fashionable society. New Yorkers, unconsciously concurring with Lu Yu's advice of a thousand years before, were very particular about the purity of the water with which they made their brew. Several springs at the outskirts of the city were well known for their particularly fine tea water. One of these, at the corner of Chatham and Roosevelt Streets, became a popular spa. At others, hawkers would fill up buckets and carry them around the city on horse carts, drawing crowds of housewives with their cries of "Tea water! Tea water!"

"Have a Cuppa Tea," a song by the English rock group, The Kinks, that eulogizes the manifold virtues of the beverage concludes with the words:

> Whatever the situation, whatever the race or creed
> Tea knows no segregation, no class nor pedigree
> It knows no motivation, no sect or organisation,
> It knows no one religion,
> Nor political belief...

Tea was a bitter drink for the unwilling Colonies.

• • • • • • • • • • • • • • • • • • •

Tea's democratic neutrality may well be one of the reasons it has remained so popular in Britain. In the Colonies, unfortunately, the leaf was drawn right to the heart of a transatlantic dispute and became, very definitely, a political symbol.

In 1765, the British government, deciding that the Colonies should help defray the cost of the French and Indian War, passed the Stamp Act, which taxed tea and other commodities. The colonists protested so fiercely that the act was repealed the following year, but in 1767 a new tax was imposed, as part of the Townshend Acts. This tax was also repealed—except for the tax on tea. The British kept the tea tax, the most important of all, simply to assert their dominion over their American territories. The enraged colonists boycotted the only legal source of tea, the British East India Company, and bought instead from Dutch smugglers. They also sought indigenous substitutes, especially one called Labradore tea. In an early example of a now all-too-familiar advertising technique, the women of New England were exhorted to:

> Throw aside your Bohea and your Green Hyson tea
> And all things with a new-fangled duty.
> Procure a good store of the choice Labradore,
> For there'll soon be enough here to suit ye.
>
> This do without fear, and to all you'll appear
> Fair, charming, true, lovely, and clever,
> Though times remain darkish young men may be
> sparkish,
> And love you much stronger than ever.

Despite such advantages, Labradore tea never caught on, but smuggled tea was so widely consumed that the British East India Company's tea sales plummeted. By 1773, the Company had such a huge surplus on their hands that they decided to force the Colonies to take it, duty and all. Thus the stage was set for America's most well known tea party.

On December 16, 1773, the Sons of Liberty met in Boston to decide what should be done with three boatloads of unwanted British tea anchored in the harbor. Sam Adams had persuaded the captain of the ships to take his cargo back to England, but the colonial governor had refused to let the ships go. At the meeting John Rowe is reputed to have asked, "Who knows how tea will mix with salt water?" Later that night, he, Paul Revere, Sam Adams, and others found out. Dressed as Mohawk Indians, they boarded the three ships and dumped a total of 342 tea chests into the harbor.

The Boston Tea Party was only the first of several similar demonstrations that greeted the arrival of British tea at New York, Philadelphia, Annapolis, and Charleston. These tea parties were in a sense manifestations of the colonists' love of the beverage but, ironically, they began the process by which tea fell from American favor.

During the revolution, American tea consumption declined, both because the beverage had been tainted by

British domination and because the turmoil of the war made it hard to come by. But Americans did not lose their fondness for the drink. The first merchant ship to sail under the flag of the United States left New York with a cargo of ginseng to be traded with the Chinese for tea. Now that America was able to trade directly with the East, tea was cheaper than it had been under the British and consumption once again began to rise. But the new federal government promptly levied a duty on tea—ranging from 15 cents a pound on black tea to 55 cents a pound for Young Hyson—a duty much higher than the 3 cents a pound that led to the War of Independence. This was a commercial blow from which the herb never really recovered.

Although tea may now rank second to coffee in the United States, it is consumed worldwide by more people and in greater quantity than any other beverage except water. England is still the world's number one consumer, importing 200,000 metric tons annually, or more than 4.5 kilograms (10 pounds) per person. The Americans occupy the second spot, importing 80,000 metric tons a year, and the Dutch, who introduced tea drinking to the Western world, are third, importing 40,000 metric tons annually.

2.
Cultivation and Commerce

ea, *Camellia sinensis*, is a flowering evergreen with leaves that range from 2.5 to 32 centimeters (1-12 inches) in length. In the wild, tea will grow into an 8-meter (26-foot) tree. It is from such trees that early Chinese tea drinkers made their beverage. They would simply go out into the woods, cut down the first tea tree they came to, and strip it of its leaves. But the beverage made from these leaves was very bitter. Early Chinese literature contains many scenes in which guests awkwardly try to excuse themselves from drinking the bitter brew that their host, with great pomp and pride, has placed before them.

Tea plants on a modern plantation are pruned continuously, so that they remain about 1 to 1.5 meters (3–5 feet) tall. At this height they are not only easier to harvest, but their leaves are far more tender and profuse than those of a full-grown tree. The tiny shoots and buds near the top of the bush make the most delicate and flavorful drink. Though the small, cream-colored flowers of the tea plant have a wonderful fragrance, they add nothing at all to the beverage and are never processed with the leaves.

All tea comes from the same species of plant. The immense variety of teas is due to differences in growing conditions, the kind of leaves harvested, and the processing technique. The tea plant is very hardy and can survive almost anywhere. It grows fastest in hot, humid, junglelike areas, where the average temperature is 32°C (85°F) and there is at least 2.5 meters (100 inches) of rain. The best tea, however, is grown between 1,200 and 1,700 meters (4,000–6,000 feet) above sea level. At these cooler altitudes, the plant matures more slowly, producing a richer, more complex leaf.

The tea plant is native to parts of India, China, and perhaps Japan. It was first used to make a beverage in China during prehistoric times, but the earliest written reference to tea-drinking was made in 350 A.D. For most of its history, China was the giant among the world's tea producers. In fact, from 1641, when Japan closed its ports to Western traders, to 1838, when the first tea crop was harvested in India, China

• • • • • • • • • • • • • • • • • • •

was the world's only tea exporter. During those years, the British East India Company, fearing that it would lose its monopoly over the tea trade, was powerful enough to stop entrepreneurs from attempting to grow tea in other parts of the world. It wasn't until the company was on the verge of collapse that extremely successful tea industries were started, not only in India, but in Ceylon (Sri Lanka) and parts of Indonesia as well. Even with the competition, China managed to produce nearly half the world's tea, growing 500 million kilograms (1,100 million pounds) annually until the late 1930s. But with World War II and the Communist revolution, Chinese tea output plunged. It now exports about 30 million kilograms (65 million pounds) a year, a mere six percent of the world's total exports.

• • • • • • • • • • • • • • • • • • •

CHINA

Most of China is ideally suited for growing tea. Its climate ranges from temperate to subtropical, and its soil, an iron-rich, sandy loam, retains moisture without becoming too wet or dry. However, China also has 800 million people to feed, so rice and other food crops have priority over tea. Tea plants are usually found only on small hillside plots that are unsuitable for other crops, or they may be planted as hedges between two fields. In some parts of China, tea plants are

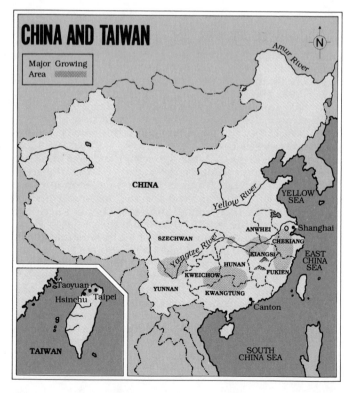

CHINA AND TAIWAN

Major Growing Area

allowed to grow in a haphazard, semiwild state, with occasional weeding or pruning.

China produces black, green, oolong, and scented teas. Because Chinese teas are classified by trade names, seasons, districts, and styles of manufacture, there are fully 8,000 different types. Fortunately, many of the variations are only used domestically, so the tea gourmet of Europe or North America has to contend with only a small fraction of the classifications. (For a more detailed discussion of the manufacturing techniques and grading systems of China and other countries, see the Gourmet Tea Buyer's Guide beginning on page 92).

There are two general types of black China teas: North China Congou (also called black leaf) and South China Congou (also called red leaf). The North Congous, which are used in the traditional English breakfast teas, are generally regarded as superior to those of the south. However, southern China produces the smoky-flavored Lapsang Souchong, which is certainly one of the world's most popular teas. The green teas of China fall into three broad categories: Hoochow, Pingsuey, and Country Green. Country Greens include all the green teas made outside the districts of Hoochow and Pingsuey. The finest Country Greens, and really the finest green teas in China, are the Moyunes, made in the Anhwei Province, west of Shanghai. Chinese oolong teas are also classified by district, but are vastly inferior to those produced in Taiwan.

● ●

JAPAN

Japan, like China, has its own thirst for tea, and consumes more of the beverage than it can afford to grow. Japan's annual tea production hovers around 100 million kilograms (200 million pounds), but exports of the crop have dwindled from about 35 million kilograms (76 million pounds) to about 2 million kilograms (4.4 million pounds) a year. At the same time, it has gradually increased its imports of tea to around 25 million kilograms (55 million pounds) a year. Japan has been growing its own tea since at least the eighth century, when Zen Buddhist priests grew the plants in their temple gardens with seeds obtained from fellow Buddhists in China. Tea was not grown commercially in Japan until after the Dutch East India Company established relations with the feudal government in 1609. Even then the tea industry took a long time to become a success. The British East India Company tried to establish a tea factory in Japan in 1621 but abandoned it two years later because of lack of demand for tea among Europeans at the time. The Dutch also built a tea factory in Japan and, perhaps because of a 50-year head start in tea marketing, found the venture profitable. Almost immediately, however, the Japanese shoguns began a campaign to isolate the island nation from contact with the western world. From about 1641 to 1859, only ships from Holland and China were permitted to enter Japanese waters, and even then there were severe limitations on what could be traded. The Japanese were so intent on isolating themselves that it was forbidden to build any boats capable of travel on the open seas.

During Japan's 218 years of seclusion, western demand for tea had grown from virtually nil to well over 45 million kilograms (100 million pounds) a year. Tea trading was big business, and European merchants had developed relatively modern expectations about the way a business should be conducted. Japan, however, had remained in the Middle Ages. Europeans had to do their trading in a tiny fishing village of only 100 families, called Yokohama. They also had to bring along plenty of silver Mexican pesos, because the Japanese had no appropriate coinage of their own. Nor did the Japaneses believe in written contracts. Business agreements were sealed with three claps of the hand, the memory of which could often fade as quickly as the sound. Needless to say, the Japanese soon caught on to modern business methods.

Japan crowds more than 100 million people onto a series of mountainous islands that, in total land mass, are smaller than the state of Wisconsin. Japanese agricultural land is scarce and a tea plant is a soil-consuming luxury. Like China, Japan tucks its tea plants into tiny plots that are of little use for anything else. Even at the peak of tea production, in the late nineteenth century, less than one-half of one percent of Japanese land was available for growing tea. However, the soil and climate are ideal for the herb, particularly in the southeastern areas where the sandy soil is kept properly moist by monsoon rains, dense fogs, and heavy dews.

Almost all of Japan's export teas are designated as *sencha*, a common tea made of tender young leaves. The finest Japanese teas are seldom found in export markets. They are the *gyokuro* (Pearl Dew) tea grown under shade to reduce the tannin content, and *tencha*, which comes from the same gardens as the gyokuro but is specially processed into a powder for use in Japanese tea ceremonies.

TAIWAN

South of Japan and east of mainland China is the island of Formosa (which means beautiful in Portuguese), on which is the country of Taiwan. Taiwan, like China and Japan, grows its tea on small plots of land that are not suitable for food crops. Nonetheless, the island exports a substantial 23 million kilograms (50 million pounds) of tea a year. The tea plants are descendants of those brought by immigrants from the mainland, who initially were only interested in producing for their own consumption. However, for reasons that are not entirely clear, Taiwan produces the world's finest and most popular oolong: the Formosa oolong. Presumably, this tea's superiority stems from the island's soil and weather conditions, but for some reason the beneficent effects of these conditions do not extend to the keemun and lapsang teas which are Taiwan's other important, though not nearly so excellent, teas.

INDIA AND SRI LANKA

India was a latecomer to commercial tea cultivation and nearly did not become a tea producer at all. An indigenous tea was found growing wild in Assam in 1823 at a time when the British East India Company was studying a proposal to grow tea in India. The idea was ultimately turned down because of fears that India tea production might endanger the Company's China tea monopoly.

Ten years later, however, conditions had changed. The East India Company's opium trafficking in China had aroused the anger of the Chinese government, and would soon lead to war. Worried that the nation's tea supply was soon to be cut off, the British Crown overrode the objections of the East India Company and backed a project to grow tea in India. Thousands of Chinese plants and seeds were brought to Assam, but they either moulded and died enroute, or refused to grow in Indian soil. The utter failure of the China tea was explained in various ways. Some people said that the Chinese boiled their seeds before letting them out of the country, others said that ignorant British officials had chosen an inferior strain of tea for the experiment, and still others maintained that since tea had been the gift of the gods to China, divine forces would prevent it from surviving outside Chinese borders. In any case, it was tea from plants native to Assam that finally took the London tea market by storm in 1838.

With the successful culture of Assam tea plants—and later hybridization of Assam and China plants—tea production in India gained stride. By 1860, at least 50 private companies had established tea enterprises in the colony, and India tea investments were the most popular attraction for London financial speculators. By the end of the nineteenth century, India surpassed China in tea exports, becoming, after 1903, the undisputed leader in international tea trade with annual exports of over 90 million kilograms (200 million pounds). In recent years, exports of India tea have pushed toward 220 million kilograms (484 million pounds), with Great Britain, the United States, and Ireland the major importers of the product.

Although it was the teas of Assam that transformed India, it is in the state of Darjeeling that the nation's finest tea is produced. Virtually all India teas are processed as black teas, and the rich Darjeeling is one of the world's best.

Sri Lanka (which was formerly Ceylon) produces the same kinds of teas as India and exports just about as much, even though its tea crop is only about half as large. However, this accomplishment is not so remarkable when you consider that Sri Lanka's population of 12 million is about two percent of India's 550 million. Per capita, the population of Sri Lanka manages to consume considerably more of its own tea than its northern neighbors do of theirs.

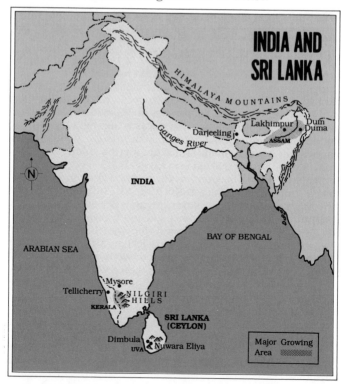

● ● ● ● ● ● ● ● ● ● ● ● ● ● ● ● ● ● ● ●

What is most remarkable, however, is the way Sri Lanka got into tea production. When the English acquired Ceylon in 1796, the island had been producing coffee on a small scale for a century. All experiments in developing tea plantations had failed, but about 100,000 hectares (250,000 acres) of cleared land produced bumper crops of coffee beans. Around 1870, however, the coffee trees of Ceylon were wiped out by a blight. Within a few years, the island's thriving coffee industry was destroyed and many coffee plantation owners were bankrupt.

Despite published reports that it could not be produced on Ceylon, a few desperate owners began planting tea on their devastated coffee plantations. Within 20 years, the tea crop grown on Ceylon's plantations was larger than the coffee crop has ever been, and additional forest land had to be cleared. Today, Sri Lanka had more than 200,000 hectares (500,000 acres) of tea plants producing beverage leaf the year around. Sri Lanka teas, most often called Ceylon teas, are generally black, and have a soft liquor. Uva and Dimbula produce very fine teas, though none of them can compare with India's best. The United States is the primary consumer of Sri Lanka's tea, much of which finds its way into tea bags and instant teas. Together, India and Sri Lanka account for at least 50 percent of all the world's export teas; in recent years, the proportion has been as high as 70 percent.

● ● ● ● ● ● ● ● ● ● ● ● ● ● ● ● ● ● ● ●

OTHER PRODUCING COUNTRIES

Although international tea trade was started in Indonesia when the Dutch East India Company built a trading base on Bantam in 1606, more than 200 years passed before tea production became profitable there. In 1684, a German naturalist and smuggler named Andres Cleyer planted some tea on Java, but only to dress up the grounds of his magnificent estate. Nonetheless, he proved that tea could be grown on the island. The Dutch East India Company became interested in starting a plantation on Java, but they were too busy competing with the British in China to give the project the time and money it required. It was not until Assam tea from India was introduced in 1878 that commercial production became feasible.

Today Indonesia, which includes Java, Sumatra, and Malaysia, is the fourth largest tea exporter in the world—45 million kilograms (100 million pounds) annually—yet it is the rare tea shop that will stock an unblended Indonesian tea. This is because Indonesia, although producing a few decent teas, produces no outstanding ones. They are marketed almost exclusively for blends. The Netherlands takes about a fourth of Indonesia's tea production, and another fourth is split between the United States and Great Britain.

Small amounts of tea, mostly for local consumption, are grown in parts of Vietnam, Thailand, and Burma. The native tribesmen of Thailand and Burma are credited by some historians as being the original tea consumers. However, they boiled the raw green leaf to make a medicinal concoction or steamed and fermented the leaves for chewing.

At least six African countries are tea producers of commercial significance: Kenya, Malawi, Mozambique, Tanzania, Uganda, and Zaire. Kenya is the largest exporter of tea among the African nations, sometimes shipping more tea than Indonesia or China. Kenya did not become a large-scale tea producer until the 1920s when experts from India inspected the soil and climates of sites outside Asia and recommended areas of Kenya as likely locations for profitable tea ventures.

Although African teas have been slow to appear in specialty stores, some high-grown products of Kenya and Uganda are of a very good quality and similar in flavor to teas of India and Sri Lanka. Uganda and Malawi each export more than 18 million kilograms (40 million pounds) annually, compared to about 45 million kilograms (100 million pounds) for Kenya, and are expanding production at a faster rate than traditional tea-growing countries. Zaire, Mozambique, and Tanzania contribute a combined total of about 45 million kilograms (100 million pounds) of tea annually.

Tea production was started in Africa in 1850 in Natal and expanded in 1877 with tea plants and workers imported from India. The Natal tea industry reached a peak production of several million pounds a year early in the twentieth century, then declined because of falling tea prices and the increased cost of imported labor.

Significant amounts of tea are produced annually in Bangladesh, Turkey, Iran, and Argentina, but little of their production enters the export market. World Bank statistics show that Turkish tea production has been growing in recent years at the fastest rate of any producing country and the country may soon become an important factor in the export tea market. Currently, Turkey produces nearly 45 million kilograms (100 million pounds) a year.

Over the past two centuries there have been attempts to grow tea commercially in Brazil, Colombia, Peru, Paraguay, Mexico, Guatemala, Jamaica, Borneo, the Philippines, the Fiji Islands, and in the Queensland area of Australia. But thus far none has been successful. Tea production was even attempted in the United States over an area stretching from Florida to Louisiana and as far north as Tennessee and North Carolina. In each case, it was found that tea could be grown—the North Carolina tea plants even survived a winter blizzard in 1851—but the high cost of labor and land makes commercial production impossible in the United States.

3.
Choosing Your Tea

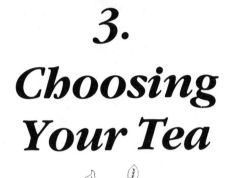

S hopping for good teas should be easier than shopping for coffees. Many of both the best unblended and blended teas are sold in small closed tins and have a long shelf life provided the containers remain tightly closed. Bulk teas, like bulk coffees, tend to lose quality faster because they are exposed to the environment. When buying bulk tea, look for the same precautions in the store as you would expect for coffee. Most important, each bin of tea should have its own airtight cover (see page 104).

TYPES AND STYLES

To get the most for your money in a gourmet tea shop, you need to know a little about how teas are plucked, manufactured, and graded.

The first stage in the manufacture is the harvest, or *plucking*, of the tea. The best leaves are the small, tender ones plucked from the growing tip of the tea bush. Sometimes a tea will be made from these tender leaves only, but more often they are mixed with all the other leaves.

Once the leaves have been plucked, they are processed in one of three ways, resulting in either green, black, or oolong teas. To make green teas, the leaves are steamed, rolled on mats, and heated. *Steaming* makes the leaves pliable and deactivates the enzymes that cause fermentation. *Rolling* breaks down the cell structure of the leaves, releasing flavorful juices. Finally, *heating* stabilizes the tea by destroying the enzymes that cause fermentation. It the tea were not heated, or *fired*, it would continue to ferment, or even rot, during shipment or while it sits on your kitchen shelf.

Fermentation is what makes black teas black and gives them their strength and rich liquor. Leaves that are to become black teas are not steamed. Instead, they are placed in a warm, moist room where they *wilt*. Wilting, sometimes called withering, allows fermentation to begin at the same time that it makes the leaves pliable. Leaves for black tea are

• • • • • • • • • • • • • • • • • • • •

rolled in much the same way as are those for green, but afterwards they are left to ferment before firing. Buyers of black tea should pay attention to its color. Contrary to what one would expect, black tea should be dark brown, sometimes with a deep-reddish tinge. If the tea is truly black, it has probably been overfired and will have a thin, weak taste.

Oolong teas are semifermented, which means that they are stronger than green teas but more delicate than black teas. Oolongs are processed much like black teas, but they are not allowed to ferment for as long.

• • • • • • • • • • • • • • • • • • • •

TEA FLAVORS

Differences in the taste of green, black, and oolong teas have a lot to do with their so-called *tannin* contents—the chemical is not really tannin, but that is what it is usually called and so, for convenience, the term will be used throughout this book.

Teas higher in tannin taste more astringent and tend to have a more pungent smell. Both of these qualities are admired, in moderation, but just how much tannin you like depends on your own taste.

In general, the less fermentation a leaf has experienced, the higher its tannin content will be: green teas tend to be highest in tannin, oolongs next, and black teas lowest. The natural tannin content of a leaf before it is fermented, however, also depends on the variety of plant, time of plucking, position of leaf on the stem, and where the plant was grown. The finest China black teas—Keemun and Ningchow—have a comparatively low tannin content, as does India's excellent Darjeeling. Assam teas, by contrast, have a very high natural tannin level. Generally speaking, the large-leaf teas of India have more tannin than do the small-leaf teas of China. Teas from Japan have a low natural tannin level, but because most of them are processed as green teas, they may end up with a higher tannin content than a China black tea. To make matters even more confusing, leaves from the same plant are lowest in tannin during March and April, with the content rising thereafter through August and September.

Tannin is not the only chemical affecting tea flavor. The volatile oils produced during fermentation add the distinctive flavors that have made black and oolong teas such favorites in the West. Lovers of black and oolong teas may object to the comparatively high tannin content and lack of oils characteristic of the best green teas. Green tea devotees may be equally scornful of the lack of both pungency and tannic bite of the other teas. If there is any general rule about tea flavors, it is that, within each of the three types of tea, the better teas have comparatively lower tannin contents. Colors, flavors, and aromas of teas are to the expert taster clues to the chemistry of the leaf being tested. Copper, for example, which can give a slight metallic taste to tea, is required for the fermentation process that is a key step in the correct

● ●

manufacture of black tea. Various amino acids and amino-acid derivates account for tea aromas; in fact, scientists have found that tea aromas can be altered by adding amino acids to tea infusions.

Because tea grows best on soils that are very acid, the acidity itself results in absorprion of certain minerals, such as aluminum and manganese, that are minor taste influences in most teas. However, concentrations of the minerals increase with the age of the leaf, just as tannin does. As a result, tea that is *tippy* (and therefore young) is likely to have different flavor characteristics than tea from leaves allowed to remain on the plant for a longer period.

Experts occasionally note differences in tea leaves that are first, second, or third *flush*, or growth. Since the tea plant is an evergreen, it has leaves year-round. But during the growing season, which varies with the geographic location, new leaves are formed periodically and are called the flush. The early flushes are likely to have a different taste than later flushes, just as the first fruits and vegetables of the season may taste better than do the same varieties picked at the end of the growing season.

Tea tasters occasionally add milk to a sample infusion to observe the changes in color and flavor that result from the combination. Some teas are manufactured for preparation with milk, and a goodly share of the world's tea drinkers take the beverage with milk. Milk contains a protein that combines with the tannins, reducing the astringent and acidity factors of the brew. Tea drinkers who add milk to tea, therefore, taste what is left once the tea's tannin has been neutralized.

● ●

WHAT'S IN A GRADE?

The next stage in the manufacturing process is the grading of the tea. Each tea is graded differently, depending on the country in which it is produced. The grades of green and oolong tea are generally related to their quality, but black teas are graded only by the size of the leaf or leaf particles. Many a buyer of black tea has been deceived by the term Orange Pekoe, which refers not to a type or flavor of tea, but only to the size of the leaf from which it is made. Orange Pekoe bears the same relation to the taste of tea as loaf-size does to the taste of bread. The size of a black tea leaf or particle only affects the speed with which it brews: the smallest grades brew fastest.

India and Sri Lanka divide their black tea grades into two main categories, one for leaves and the other for particles. The leaf grades, in descending order of size, are Souchong, Pekoe, and Orange Pekoe. The particle grades, also in descending order, are Broken Pekoe Souchong, Broken Pekoe, Broken Orange Pekoe, Fannings, and Dust. The last two grades are very small and brew very quickly. They are typically used only by institutions or caterers, who need to make large amounts of tea.

● ● ● ● ● ● ● ● ● ● ● ● ● ● ● ● ● ● ●

PROFESSIONAL TASTER'S GLOSSARY

The following guide to the terms used by professional tasters will help the reader understand descriptions of tea both in this book and at the retail shop.

Agony of the Leaves. The unfolding of the tea leaves when boiling water is applied to them.

Baggy. An undesirable aroma caused when the tea leaf is withered on an oriental-type of cloth called hessian, a burlap that imparts its odor to the tea.

Bakey. A tea leaf that has been overcooked during the firing process so that too much moisture was driven from the leaf. Bakey tea lacks sparkle and mellowness.

Biscuity. A yeasty aroma sometimes noted in a well-fired black tea from Assam.

Body. A liquor that has strength and fullness. The opposite is a beverage that is thin.

Bright. An infusion that has a sparkling red color, sometimes described as resembling polished copper.

Brisk. A beverage that feels lively to the palate, with a degree of pungency. A brisk taste usually is a characteristic of a tea that has been properly fired.

Brownish. A color characteristic of tea but not always related to the quality of the beverage. Some tea leaves, particularly tippy tea, have a natural brownish coloration. However, tea that has been fired at excessively high temperatures after inadequate withering also has a brownish coloring.

Coppery. See Bright.

Dull. An infusion that lacks clarity and brightness in visual appearance and a sign of a poor-quality beverage resulting from faulty processing of the leaf.

Flaky. A flat, open tea leaf, and a sign of a poorly processed tea or a tough leaf that resisted processing. Improper plucking, withering, or rolling, and toughness, or a combination of those factors, results in flaky tea.

Flat. A negative aroma and flavor characteristic in a tea that lacks pungency, briskness, and flavor.

Gone Off. A tea that has deteriorated in quality because it is old,

China, Java, and Sumatra also use these grades, but China adds a grade called Flowery Pekoe, and Java and Sumatra add one called Flowery Orange Pekoe. These terms indicate the presence of very young tea leaves that can, but don't always, give the tea a superior taste.

Green teas are graded according to age and style of leaf, both of which affect the taste of the tea. The Chinese grades, ordered from best to worst, run as follows:

Gunpowder. Young or medium-aged tea leaves rolled into tiny balls.

Young Hyson. Medium-aged leaves, long and thinly rolled or twisted.

Imperial. Loosely balled remains of Gunpowder, generally made from older leaves.

Hyson. Old leaves twisted in the style of Young Hyson.

Twankay. Old, open leaves; poor quality.

Hyson Skin. Even poorer quality than Twankay.

Dust. Whatever is left at the bottom of the bin.

tainted, or moldy. A high moisture content often contributes to tea deterioration in storage.

Hard. A pronounced pungency that is preferred in black tea from Assam.

Harsh. A raw, bitter characteristic of a tea that has not been withered properly. The harshness is caused by the presence of chemicals, called polyphenols, that normally are altered by the withering process to eliminate the bitterness.

High-Fired. A tea that has been dried at very high exhaust temperature without actually burning or scorching the leaf. High-fired tea resists deterioration but loses pungency and flavor in the processing.

Malty. A tea that has a faint aroma of malt, a desirable characteristic found in some tea that has been moderately high-fired.

Mixed. Leaves of an unblended tea that appears to be composed of several varieties because leaf colors are not uniform. This is a sign that the tea that has been poorly manufactured, the diverse colors resulting from uneven withering and fermentation.

Muddy. The opposite of bright when applied to the clarity of the liquor of a freshly infused tea. However, a good-quality liquor can develop an opaque appearance after standing and cooling because of chemical changes in the infusion.

Plain. A liquor that has no particular pungency, quality, or other desirable characteristics. A plain tea may also have a sour taste.

Pungent. A sharp, astringent effect on the palate, but more acrid than bitter.

Round. Good strength and color without harshness.

Self-Drinking. A tea that has enough flavor, aroma, and body to be drunk as an unblended tea.

Tainted. A tea that has acquired an undesirable aroma or flavor because of contamination by a microorganism during manufacturing or storage. Tea also may acquire bad flavor through storage or shipment in an environment contaminated by a strong odor such as onions or kerosene.

Tippy. A tea with golden bud leaves, usually meaning that leaves are young. Silver or white tips are a sign of overwithering or other damage during manufacture.

Woody. An undesirable flavor characteristic that can give tea the taste of grass or hay.

Green Japanese teas are classified by processing methods (pan-fired, basket-Fired, etc.) and by style of leaf (curled leaf, natural leaf), but these labels have no relation to quality. The quality ratings, from best to worst, are Extra Choicest, Choicest, Choice, Finest, Fine, Good, Medium, Good Common, Nibs, Fannings, and Dust.

India's green tea grades are Fine Young Hyson, Young Hyson, Hyson Number One, Twankay, Sowmee, Fannings, and Dust.

Oolong tea is graded strictly according to quality: Choice, Finest to Choice, Finest, Fine to Finest, Fine Up, Fine, On Fine, Superior to Fine, Superior Up, Fully Superior, Superior, On Superior, Good to Superior, Good Up, Fully Good, On Good, and Standard.

• • • • • • • • • • • • • • • • • •

THE GOURMET BUYER'S GUIDE

The following list is provided to help you become familiar with some of the better teas found in gourmet and specialty shops. Technical terms used in the entries are explained in the Taster's Glossary on page 90. But it is important to remember that no tea ever tastes alike for any two people, and that no matter how highly recommended a particular leaf or blend may come, its true goodness is, in the words of the master, Lu Yu, a decision for the mouth to make. The three kinds of straight tea are listed separately, followed by the blended and scented teas.

• • • • • • • • • • • • • • • • • •

UNBLENDED BLACK TEAS

Assam. A fine malty tea that has evolved from a variety found growing wild in the Assam province of northeastern India in the 1830s. The best Assam tea, which is noted for its full, rich, pungent characteristics, is produced in Lakhimpur and Dum Duma. Assam teas from Dooars is thick-liquoring and tastes very much like Darjeeling. Assam tea generally is very good in quality and relatively easy to find. Even a less than perfect Assam is in great demand for use in the more expensive blends.

Ceylon. The general name for tea produced in Sri Lanka. The plant is a close relative of the Assam indigenous tea plant that is the ancestor of most of the teas of India, Sri Lanka, and Kenya. While most Ceylon tea yields a strong beverage with good flavor, factors other than leaf size are more important: a leaf that is large because of its age may be tough, leathery, and inferior in quality.

Ching Wo. Regarded as the best South China (red leaf) Congou, Ching Wo is produced in the Fujian Province of the People's Republic of China. It has a tightly rolled, silky leaf with a delicate aroma. The infusion shows a bright reddish color with considerable body and an excellent flavor that is so distinctive it can often be detected in black tea blends.

Darjeeling. A type of mountain-grown tea produced along the slopes of the Himalaya Mountains in northeast India at elevations of up to 1,900 meters (6,500 feet) above sea level. It is the finest tea grown in India and one of the finest in the world. Whereas Assam tea is sometimes identified as malty in flavor, Darjeeling is characterized by a nutty taste. It also is consistently full-bodied with a rich, red liquor and delicious taste that other tea cannot duplicate. Because of the distinctive flavor of Darjeeling tea, leaf size is a less important consideration. However, the pluckings made in June and October are usually the best. Gold-Tip Darjeeling is a very fine style of Darjeeling tea, composed mainly of young shoots. The Darjeeling tips are long, twisted, and golden. While tips do not significantly affect flavor in Darjeeling tea, their presence is a sign of quality manufacturing, since producers who think in terms of quantity rather than quality usually do not preserve the tips.

Flowery Orange Pekoe. A special grade of tea used in China and Indonesia to designate masses of Pekoe tips, very young leaves that turn a light color when fermented and fired. A tippy tea may be quite delicate in flavor, but cannot improve a tea that has flat flavor to begin with. A Flowery Orange Pekoe may be quite neutral or even poor as an unblended tea, depending on what plants it comes from. If possible, try before you buy.

Keemun Congou. One of the best of the northern China black teas. Keemun tea has a rich aroma and yields a full, thick, almost sappy beverage. Keemun tea originally was common green tea until it was discovered that when allowed to ferment, the leaves produced a drink so fine that it has been termed the burgundy of China teas. Keemun Congou is used in some English breakfast blends.

Kenya. A black tea usually produced from high-grown plants originally imported from India. The leaves yield a rich aroma and brisk, delicate flavor in the cup. Kenya is the world's third largest exporter of black teas, many closely resembling the black tea of India and Sri Lanka.

Lapsang Souchong. One of the best known of the South China Congous. Souchong is a name applied to certain large-leaf grades of black tea from China, India, Sri Lanka, and Indonesia. The Lapsang Souchong—a variety that originated in Fujian Province —is very black, large, and has a slightly curled leaf. The liquor produced during infusion is rich, syrupy, and smoky. Some describe the flavor as pleasantly tarlike. Lapsang Souchong makes an exciting unblended tea, and its aroma can be detected in some expensive blends. In fact, the aroma of Lapsang Souchong can drift into other teas and food items and should therefore be isolated in its own airtight container.

Orange Pekoe. A grade of black tea that varies widely in quality according to the country of origin, the elevation at which the tea was grown, the climate at the time it was grown, and the method by which the leaf was processed after being plucked. The term is believed to have originated from the name of a China tea processed from the earliest pluckings of the season and flavored with the scent of orange blossoms. The U.S. Department of Agriculture once set specifications for teas that can be identified as Orange Pekoes, but amendments and interpretations have rendered the term virtually meaningless except to identify it as a leaf that is too large to fall through a sieve with a specific mesh size. The words Orange Pekoe on a label have about the same significance as the words drip grind on a container of ground coffee.

Russian. A tea grown in the Transcaucasian region of the U.S.S.R., mainly in Azerbaidzhan and the Georgian S.S.R. The tea plantations were established by the Tsars in the nineteenth century, and most of the annual production is consumed domestically. However, small amounts of Russian tea are exported to European countries, finding their way into specialty stores around the world. It is a long-leaf tea with characteristics similar to those of the China teas that were the ancestors of the Russian plantings. The cup quality is likely to be thin and light, and may taste best when served in the Russian manner—with a slice of lemon. This tea should not be confused with the full-bodied Russian blends such as Russian Caravan tea.

Yunnan. Tea from this province in southwestern China was first exported over 1,000 years ago. Originally a source of green tea, Yunnan in recent years has developed a black tea that is lighter and more delicately flavored than some of the traditional South China Congous.

UNBLENDED GREEN TEAS

Chun Mee. A type of China green tea made from small, hard, twisted Young Hyson leaves that, in turn, are made from young to medium-age leaves. Chun Mee, also spelled Chunmee, is one of the favorite China teas transplanted to Taiwan by Chinese immigrants, and the Chun Mee sold in most specialty and gourmet shops today comes from Taiwan rather than China. Since Chun Mee is a grade and style of leaf rather than a quality indicator, it is hard to determine at a distance whether any Chun Mee per se will yield a memorable beverage. A good quality Chun Mee should be crisply dry and have an aroma of fresh vegetables. Like all green teas other than Gunpowder, Chun Mee has a tendency to become stale quickly if exposed to the air.

Dragon Well. A China green tea that is one of the finest available for use as an unblended green, it is quite popular but rather scarce. It is produced in Chekiang Province, near the East China Sea, the source of the best Country Greens. Dragon Well is marked by clearness and a rich, delicate, toasty flavor. The aroma of fresh Dragon Well should be pleasantly herbaceous.

Gunpowder. This is another case where a brand name refers only to a grade of tea, but here the name does indicate quality. Gunpowder Tea is manufactured by a process in which each tea leaf is rolled into a small pellet. Young tea leaves are generally used, and the smaller the pellets, the more expensive the tea. A top grade of Gunpowder Tea in China is composed of very tiny pellets. A lower grade consists of loosely rolled leaves. The Chinese name for Gunpowder Tea is Siaou Chu, which literally means large leaf. Gunpowder Green/Imperial is a China green tea made from older leaves. In Chinese, Gunpowder Green/Imperial may be called Ta Chu, which means large rolled leaf. In general, Gunpowder Tea offers a subtle fragrance and a sweet, pungent flavor.

Rolling the leaf has two effects on the quality of the product. It forces to the surface flavorful juices that otherwise would remain inside the leaf. Rolling also forces out water, thus helping to reduce the tea's final moisture content. The pellet retains its shape during firing and keeps its freshness longer than tea not manufactured in pellet form.

Gyokuru. A sweet-tasting tea from the fields around Uji, it is the finest produced in Japan. It is made by a special process from plants in shaded gardens. Only the tender top buds of the plants are plucked for Gyokuru, which means "pearl dew," and special care is taken to prevent bruising, which might result in a small amount of fermentation. Steaming, rolling, and firing are done by hand rather than by machine. The result is a tea with increased caffeine content but lower levels of tannins. Its sweet, delicate flavor has earned Gyokuru the title of the white wine of teas. However, less than one percent of Japanese green tea is Gyokuru, and most Gyokuru is consumed domestically. Because of the special care given the leaf from growing to finishing, Gyokuru is expensive, but for tea lovers who like to go first class, the experience is worth the cost.

Pingsuey. A China green tea from Chekiang Province, varying in cup quality with the harvest. First-crop Pingsuey is light-liquoring, sweet-flavored, and sea green in the cup. Later crops are likely to have poorer cup quality and a metallic taste. Pingsuey tea is produced in several districts but is called Pingsuey for the name of the market town where it is sold.

Young Hyson. Another tea whose name refers only to its grade, it consists of young to medium-aged leaves manufactured in a thinly rolled, long, twisted style that resembles twisted thread. The Chinese name for Young Hyson is Yu Chin Ch'a. Chun Mee is a grading subdivision of Young Hyson. This tea was so popular during the eighteenth century that English law placed a higher import duty on it than on any other tea.

Yunnan Tipped. A tea made from the bud leaves of tea produced in China's Yunnan Province. The tippy leaf is a characteristic of the finer teas produced in the newly developed districts of Yunnan. While tipped tea usually indicates the use of the younger, tender leaves of a plant, younger leaves of one tea plant are not necessarily superior to the older leaves of another plant. Yunnan Tipped tea should make a fine beverage, but try before you buy.

UNBLENDED OOLONG TEAS

Black Dragon. The English translation of oolong is Black Dragon. The name may be applied to any semifermented tea that has been hand-rolled and heated to dryness over a charcoal fire. Until Formosa oolong entered the market around the end of the nineteenth century, nearly all oolong tea was shipped from Amoy and Canton, China. During the early years of Formosa oolong production, its oolong tea was shipped to Amoy to be exported with China oolong.

Formosa Oolong. The best oolong tea and one of the finest teas of any kind, marked by a piquant pungency and an almost fruity flavor in the cup. The superiority of Formosa oolong is an accident due in part to the natural climate and soil of Taiwan. Oolong originated in the Fujian Province of China and was transplanted to Taiwan by immigrants who missed the tea of their native region on the mainland. Once transplanted to Formosan soil, oolong proved so fine that it became the oolong of choice throughout the world. Taiwan produces five crops of oolong between April and December. The second and third harvests produce the best tea.

Mainland Oolong. China oolong tea tends to be rough in comparison to Formosa oolong yet it can be brisk and rich in flavor. It all depends upon the area in which it is produced and the period of harvest: like Formosa oolong, that of the mainland is harvested four to five times a year, with the summer crops yielding the finest tea.

BLENDED TEAS

Listed below are traditional blends that have survived over centuries. If you cannot find or don't enjoy reputable packaged blends, you can blend teas yourself using the information given in the list.

Chinese Restaurant. This blend may vary somewhat according to local preferences. A typical Chinese Restaurant blend contains about 50 percent Formosa or China black or oolong tea. The other 50 percent consists of a mixture of a China green tea and a jasmine-scented tea.

Dragonmoon. A blend of full-bodied Darjeeling and thick, rich Assam tea.

English Breakfast. Originally, this blend was composed of northern China congou, such as Keemuns, but today's English Breakfast Tea is more likely to be a mixture of India and Ceylon black tea. It is a strong blend, good to get you going in the morning and typically served with milk and sugar.

French Blend. A combination that usually contains four parts China black tea to one part India or Ceylon tea. Four parts Lapsang Souchong to one part Darjeeling is a common variety.

Irish Breakfast Tea. A brisk, strong blend of Assam and Ceylon tea, and, like English Breakfast Tea, quite compatible with milk and sugar.

Lady Londonderry. A blend of black tea from India, Sri Lanka, and Taiwan, developed for a famed hostess of the same name.

Prince of Wales. A blend of northern China congou, with a thick, sappy liquor and a rich aroma and flavor.

Queen Mary Blend. A combination of choice Darjeeling tea, containing mainly Orange Pekoe grades.

Russian Blend. A traditional Russian mixture of China black tea, composed of three parts Lapsang Souchong to one part northern China congou and one part southern China congou. The northern China leaf is usually a Ningchow, which is similar to a Keemun but lighter in body, and the southern China congou may be a red-leaf Paklum. The Russian blend may also contain one part China Orange Pekoe instead of a congou.

Russian Caravan. A combination of black tea that varies according to the dealer who packages it. One Russian Caravan Tea contains northern China congou and Formosa oolong, reportedly blended for the Russian aristocracy in a period before Formosa produced oolong tea. Another Russian Caravan formula consists of 60 percent Keemun, 30 percent Darjeeling, and the remainder a mixture of oolong and Flowery Pekoe.

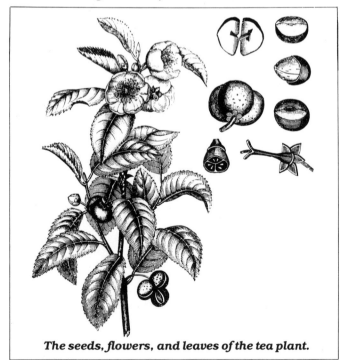

The seeds, flowers, and leaves of the tea plant.

HOW MUCH CAFFEINE IN TEA

Tea variety	Caffeine content* (as % of dry weight)
Japan Green (average)	2.0–3.3%
China Green	2.0–3.7%
Japan Sencha	2.5–3.2%
Java Black	2.7–4.4%
Ceylon Black	2.73–4.1%
Japan Gyokuro	3.0–4.0%
African Black	3.10–3.11%
Taiwan Oolong	3.1–3.7%
India Black	3.26–3.35%

*The caffeine content of tea leaves varies with age of the leaves, the youngest leaves being the lowest in caffein.

SCENTED/SPICED TEAS

Black Currant. A fine black tea, such as a Darjeeling, is often improved when scented with black currant essence.

Caper. A highly pungent China black tea scented with clove oil, caper tea is so-called because the rolled tea leaves resemble capers.

Cardamom. A botanical cousin of ginger, cardamom makes a compatible aromatic combination with fine black tea.

Chrysanthemum. These blossoms are used to scent tea, creating Chrysanthemum Tea. The blossoms are scattered on beds of hot, just-fired tea leaves, forming layers of tea separated by layers of blossoms. The blossoms may be removed several hours later, or mixed permanently with the tea leaves.

Cinnamon. A common ingredient in spiced tea, available in packaged blends. You can also add it at home to your own favorite tea, by adding a one-and-a-half inch stick of cinnamon to one cup of black tea.

Constant Comment. The trade name of a tea flavored with the scent of oranges.

Earl Grey. The essential identifier in this common tea is the scent of oil of bergamot, a citrus fruit. Originally, the name was applied only to a bergamot-scented China black tea, but in recent years it has been used as a label for a number of different black tea blends with the bergamot scent. A delightful afternoon tea.

Jamaica Ginger. A spiced tea flavored with ginger, sold as a pre-packaged tea. It can also be spiced at home with dried, crystallized, or candied ginger, in a proportion of one slice fresh or candied root to 2 cups of black tea.

Jasmine Blossom. A tea scented with jasmine blossoms, produced by the same method used for Chrysanthemum tea. Jasmine Blossom tea is usually made with Hyson green tea leaves or a blend of Hyson and black tea.

Lemon, Lime, Orange. Teas in which the scent is provided by the dried rind or fruit of lemon, lime, or orange.

Lychee. A tea that is scented with the aroma of lychee blossoms. The lychee scent is acquired by growing the tea plants and lychee trees in the same garden rather than by layering flower blossoms and fired tea leaves together, as is done in Jasmine or Chrysanthemum teas.

Mint. A black or green tea flavored with either peppermint or spearmint. The mint may be added as a fresh or dried leaf.

Pouchong. An oolong produced in China and Taiwan, that is scented before the final firing with gardenia, jasmine, or yulan (a type of magnolia) blossoms.

Rose. A black tea with rose petals layered into it. Rose tea is popular in Indian restaurants. It should not be confused with rose hips tea (see page 125).

Star Anise. A tea flavored with the seed of oil of an Oriental magnolia, also known as Chinese anise, but not related to the licorice-flavored member of the carrot family. The star anise lends a flavor reminiscent of cloves or cinnamon, but less pungent than either.

4.

Making Tea

The first Chinese tea drinkers had no teapots. The earliest records of tea making indicate that in the fourth century tea was made by boiling the leaves in a primitive kettle. Lu Yu, in his *Ch'a Ching* classic of 780 A.D., advises that tea be made in the cup. The *Ch'a Ching* contains an illustration of a teapot, but the utensil also has been identified as a wine jug with a very narrow spout that probably would have been impractical for infusing tea. Among other hazards, the tea leaves probably would have clogged the spout.

TEAPOTS

In the sixteenth century, an unknown potter in a Yangtze River town of Ihing, or Yi-Hsing, began making stoneware pots with large mouths that eliminated the problem of tea-leaf clogging. They were called *boccarros*, or large mouth, by the early Portuguese explorers. The first teapots to reach Europe were mostly simple, primitive earthenware pots, although some were made in the shapes of animals, fruits, and vegetables.

Teapots have remained essentially unchanged for nearly 400 years. An Ihing pot of the Ming Dynasty would not look out of place on your dining-room table today. What variations there have been from the design of the Ihing pot were made for practical reasons. The Japanese, for example, have moved the handle closer to the top of the pot to make it easier to carry. In Tibet, where tea is commonly churned with yak cream, the pot has a wider top opening and wider spout, for easier mixing and pouring of the milk-shake-thick drink.

The Europeans and Americans now make their teapots according to the oriental design, but they didn't always. The first western pots were heavy, awkward, ugly things because the clay used by European potters could not stand up to sudden changes in temperature unless it was very thick and well glazed. The Dutch developed a delftware pot, finished in

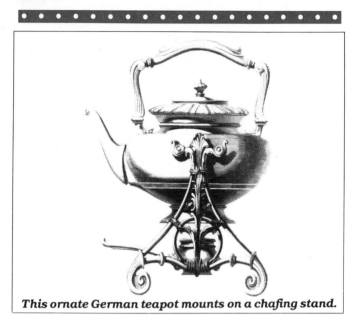

This ornate German teapot mounts on a chafing stand.

a whitish tin glaze, that looked like its Chinese models, but it would shatter when hot water was poured into it on a cold day. The most practical and beautiful European pots of the early seventeenth century were made of silver and other metals; however, since metal is such a good conductor of heat, the tea in these pots had to be consumed quickly or it would get cold. It wasn't until the end of the seventeenth century that clay suitable for making thin-walled ceramic pots was discovered in Staffordshire, England.

During the eighteenth century the manufacturing of teaware became a creative and competitive business. Josiah Wedgwood was the genius of the age. His cream-colored queen's ware and his delicate blue and white jasperware are among the finest examples of the potter's art ever made in Europe. It was during this age, as well, that Josiah Spode first introduced bone china, and created a new fashion in teaware.

Perhaps the most significant advance of the eighteenth century was the development of a technique for manufacturing ceramic pots from molds. This allowed potters to mold their clay into far more varied and complicated shapes than had ever been possible on the traditional potter's wheel. Teapots could be shaped like elephants with the trunk raised as a spout. Or the spout might be designed as a snake with its mouth open and the rest of its body coiled about a fat Oriental man sitting on a cushion. A particularly interesting eighteenth-century saltglaze teapot was made in the shape of a girl riding a goose, with the neck and head of the goose serving as the spout.

However, despite all their elegant and fanciful ornamentation, the teapots of the eighteenth century suffered from a rather basic mechanical problem: their tops fell off. It wasn't until the nineteenth century that an unknown inventor developed a teapot lid with little protrusions on its lip that could fit through slots and then be twisted around under the lip of the pot, thereby keeping it secure when the pot was tipped over to pour out the last drops of tea.

The people of the nineteenth century were, on the whole, more interested in adding mechanical contrivances to their teapots than in decorating them. Not all of these contrivances were as practical as the locking lid. In 1835, a patent was issued for a cast-iron insert that could be heated up and then placed into a teapot to keep the tea warm. A merchant's wife in Bristol, England, invented a teapot with a suspended wire basket for boiling eggs while making tea. An American inventor patented a teapot with a plunger for squeezing the last drops of flavor from the leaves at the bottom.

The metal tea ball was invented during this period, and with it came a device that would automatically lift it out of the tea after a given number of minutes. One such device was controlled by a tiny hourglass mechanism from which water dropped until a float was released to raise the leaves above the beverage. An American named Caleb Morales patented a teapot lid with a built-in clockwork timer that raised the tea ball into a hollow space in the lid after a fixed number of minutes.

An electric teapot patented in England in 1909 not only heated the water to boiling but contained a steam-operated mechanism that opened a trap and allowed dry tea leaves to fall into the water when it was boiling. And if any reader is thinking of inventing a cube-shaped teapot, it has already been done. In 1916, an inventor in England, R.C. Johnson, patented a teapot called the Cube, claiming that it was safer to handle and store because of its six flat sides.

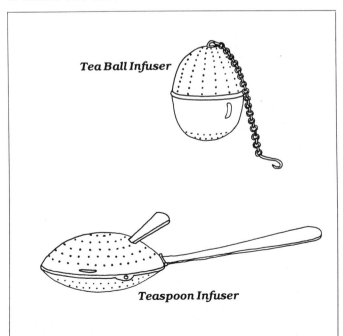

Tea Ball Infuser

Teaspoon Infuser

● ●

Modern teapots are still manufactured according to the old designs. Since a teapot really only serves to contain the leaves and water while they are brewing, its chief virtues are passive. It should keep the tea hot and it should be convenient for pouring. Metal pots are to be avoided, since they conduct heat and can lend an unpleasant flavor to the tea. Glass and ceramic teapots should be designed so that the handle on the lid and the pot handle don't burn your hand. Too many teapots allow insufficient clearance between handle and pot; burned knuckles result. It is also a good idea to make sure that your teapot's top has a tongue to keep it from falling off the pot when you pour out the last drops.

Today, many people prefer to use a teapot with an infuser that keeps the tea leaves in a separate, perforated container. This prevents tea leaves from getting into the cup, and allows you to remove the leaves from the pot as soon as the tea has been steeped to your taste. The finest infuser teapots, like the popular French Jenaer, artfully combine the infuser and the pot, but a metal tea ball, or tea egg, in an ordinary pot will do just as well. Tea balls in the shape of spoons are available for those who want to make only one cup at a time.

For all the convenience an infuser may offer, some people hold to the notion that a simple, brown stoneware English teapot is unsurpassed for keeping tea hot. What if a few leaves get into the teacup, they argue. You can use them to tell your fortune.

● ●

TEACUPS

Teacups have changed less in design over the years than teapots. The original teacup was a small bowl. The small teabowls used in some oriental restaurants today are remarkably similar to the serving vessels shown in the *Ch'a Ching* in 780 A.D. According to the *Ch'a Ching* recipes for tea making, the amount of water required for five cups of tea was one *sheng*, equivalent to a pint in the English system. Thus, each of the cups could hold approximately three ounces of tea, or about half the amount ordinarily served in a modern teacup. Tea and coffee were relatively expensive commodities in Europe until large plantations were developed in the Orient and Latin America, so servings were very small and there was no demand for tea sets with cups larger than those used in ancient China.

Oriental teacups underwent a slight modification in design after tea culture became established in Japan. The Zen Buddhists of Japan established some standards for the utensils employed in the preparation and serving of tea, including certain recommendations relating to teacups. The Chinese teacups were found to be acceptable but not ideal, because of their hard appearance. However, a humble Korean rice bowl that had been adapted for tea-drinking was favored because its lack of symmetry made it look softer and less formal. Although too wide and flat for proper tea-drinking, the Korean rice bowl was modified to a proper thickness, one

Infuser Teapot

that would retain warmth and yet not become too hot to hold comfortably. And by giving the bowl a cylindrical shape, the tea whisk of the tea ceremony could be used without the danger of whisking tea out of the cup. The style became known a *raku*.

To most Westerners, all oriental teabowls may look alike, but for the serious Oriental tea-drinker, there are subtle variations in design that are related to different uses. A large teabowl, for example, is used for *koicha*, or thick tea, while a smaller teabowl is used for serving *usucha*, or thin tea. The difference between thick tea and thin tea is that thin tea is made from leaves so light they can be made to float away from the others by waving a fan over a stack of freshly dried tea leaves. A deep teabowl is used for winter tea-drinking, while protocol dictates that summer tea-drinking should be done from a shallow bowl.

Cups with handles were already in use in Europe when tea made its entry: the English used a two-handled cup for drinking a mixture of spiced and sweetened milk, curdled with ale or wine, called posset. Posset was served hot, so the English potters had some previous experience in manufacturing ceramic cups for hot drinks. The first European teacups, therefore, were adapted from the hot posset cups.

Early in the eighteenth century, the Russians and some of their neighbors began drinking tea from glasses instead of cups. However, because of the difficulty of holding a glass of hot tea, cuplike metal teaglass holders were developed. Tea-drinkers of the Middle East also began taking their tea in glasses, although the teaglasses of the Middle East were of demitasse or espresso size, whereas the Russian-style tea-glass is a full-sized tumbler. As the teapots and teacups of western Europe became a new medium upon which artists could paint imaginative pictures, the Russian teaglass

● ●

holder became a metallic canvas for brilliant enameled designs and illustrations.

The Russians solved the problem of how to hold a vessel of boiling hot liquid without discomfort by designing metal teaglass holders, but the ceramic-cup users had to develop another scheme to avoid finger burns. Why not invent a small ceramic plate in a design to match the cup? Around 1800, the English potters introduced the cup plate, which we now know by the name of saucer. Actually, the idea of a teacup holder was not that new. Lu Yu's *Ch'a Ching* had recommended a thousand years earlier that the teacup should be placed in a wooden lacquered cup holder to avoid burning the hands.

For reasons not entirely clear, the popularity of teacup holders has waxed and waned over the centuries. After being revived as cup plates in the early nineteenth century, saucers fell into disuse again. Interest in the game of bridge is credited with sparking renewed popularity, because the saucer made it safer to serve drinks during the game.

● ●

STORING TEA

Theoretically, one pound of tea should yield up to 300 cups of beverage, almost a year's supply at the rate of one cup per day. Since the shelf life of loose tea is approximately two years—if it is kept in an airtight container—one should not worry about ever running out of fresh tea.

Realistically, while tea does not decline as rapidly in aroma and flavor as roasted coffee, some teas will suffer more rapidly from exposure to the moisture, oxygen, and warmth of the kitchen. Green teas, other than gunpowder, are generally the most sensitive to staling. Indeed, some green teas are refired before export to prevent flavor decay. Gunpowder teas are longer lived, because the tightly rolled leaves resist effects of air and humidity. If fact, gunpowder teas often retain their freshness longer than certain of the black teas. The most aromatic of black teas, such as Darjeelings, are the more susceptible to decline in quality.

All teas should be stored in dry, airtight containers. The kinds that come in small tins are adequately protected. Save any empty tins to store the teas you buy in bulk. If you lack airtight tins, store the teas in clean, dry plastic or glass containers. Make sure that a reused tin or jar is free of odor and residue. Strong tea odors, like those of Lapsang Souchong, can take over a weaker tea.

Do not keep the teas close to onions, spices or other foods that are highly aromatic, either. Unlike coffee, teas should be stored in a cool but not cold, dry environment. Do not keep teas in refrigerators or food freezers as these kitchen conveniences are prime sources of the condensed moisture which can hasten the decline of tea flavor.

The same general rules apply to tea bags, except that tea bags, even in an airtight container, have a slightly shorter shelf life than loose teas. Otherwise, there is no reason to despise the tea bag providing it contains a fine tea.

● ●

FIVE STEPS TO
A GOOD CUP OF TEA

1. Fill tea kettle to correct level with fresh, cold water. Bring to rolling boil.

2. Heat teapot with fresh, hot water.

3. Empty teapot and add tea, measuring out 1 rounded teaspoon per cup. When making 6 or more cups, add 1 teaspoon "for the Pot."

4. Pour boiling water into teapot and allow to steep for three minutes.

5. Remove infuser or transfer tea to fresh pot, to prevent oversteeping.

● ●

JAPANESE TEA CEREMONY

For more than 400 years, the Japanese tea ceremony, or *cha no yu*, has been performed following the same 37 steps that govern every move in the ritual from the arrival of the guests to the washing of the cups. In some phases of the ceremony, the guests may compliment the host or hostess for the food items as each is served in turn and, also as part of the ritual, the principal guest may apologize to the others for taking the first cup of tea. The guests also may offer a compliment to the host or hostess in a sort of toast before drinking the tea. However, purists insist that the only sounds during the ceremony should be those of the utensils touching each other as the tea is prepared and served.

There are numerous details of behavior during the ceremony that must be observed, such as lifting the bowl of tea with the right hand, turning the bowl so the front does not face the guest, wiping the part of the rim that the guest has touched with his or her lips, and so on. The guests may or may not ask questions about the utensils and inspect their craftsmanship, although in some ceremonies it would be impolite to avoid this courtesy.

The actual ceremony usually begins with the serving of cakes. The cakes may be dry cakes or wet cakes, or both, depending upon whether the tea is prepared with thick or thin powdered tea. Dry cakes often are made with a colored rice-jelly mixture pressed into special shapes and served on a tray. Wet cakes are served from a cake dish. The guest takes a piece of cake and places it on a paper napkin. It is customary to use the fingers when eating the cakes.

The tea is prepared by the host or hostess while the guests are eating the food. The powdered tea is measured in a proportion of two scoops of powdered tea for each bowl of water. The tea is whisked with a utensil designed for that purpose, a whisk made from a single piece of bamboo finely divided into loops at the end. The tea is whisked in a back-and-forth motion, moving the arm from the shoulder. When the tea is ready, the guest who has already been identified as the principal guest takes the first bowl.

As venerable as the tea ceremony may seem, it is based on a

much older Chinese ceremony. The eighth-century volume, *Ch'a Ching*, outlined the proper procedures for selecting the leaves of the tea plant, the exact manner in which the leaves were to be baked and pulverized, the type of spring water to be added to the processed leaves, and the precise sounds one must listen for when bringing the water to each of the three boiling stages. The author Lu Yu's code of tea preparation described exactly the equipment to be used when making a proper cup of tea, including the brush for cleaning the pot and the towel for wiping the cups after each use.

The Lu Yu code was such an important ritual that it could not be entrusted to women. It was performed by the male head of the household, with certain servants permitted to assist in such crucial tasks as holding the pot of boiling water.

More than 500 years elapsed between the publication of the *Ch'a Ching* and the establishment of the Japanese tea ceremony. During that half millenium, the Zen Buddhist monks—active in both China and Japan—maintained a daily tea ceremony that bridged the gap between Lu Yu's ritual and the comparatively recent Japanese tea ceremony. The Zen monks maintained in their monasteries a room or area of a room similar to a chapel where they regularly gathered to drink a ceremonial bowl of tea before the image of Bodhidharma, founder of the Zen sect. The chapel area, which the Japanese called the *tokonoma*, gradually came to be included in secular architecture as well as a reception room that could be closed off from the rest of the house by a screen. In aristocratic Japanese homes, tea was soon served to guests in the *tokonoma*, which would also be decorated with paintings and fresh flowers.

At the time of the Shogun Yoshimasa, in the late fifteenth century, houses began to be built with a separate tearoom or tea chamber. The first private tearoom in Japan may have been built for Yoshimasa's own retirement home, the famous Silver Pavillion near Kyoto. When the Shogun retired, he invited a Zen priest named Shuko to visit the home. Shuko suggested that a whole room be set aside as a *tokonama* for tea ceremonies: the Shogun became so intrigued with the ceremony that he became deeply involved in tea-drinking rituals, collecting tea utensils and inviting important people to ceremonies, and honoring Shuko by appointing him director of the *chanoyu* ceremonies.

According to the story, Shuko did not have all the details about the original tea ceremonies, so his own code was based on word-of-mouth information he obtained from others who could recall bits of the *Ch'a Ching* code. (One major difference in the *cha no yu* is that a special powdered tea, called *mattcha*, is used.)

Around 1588, the *cha no yu* was further refined at a congress of Zen tea masters held near Kyoto. All the leaders of the ceremony from various temples throughout Japan were ordered to attend the sessions under penalty of being forbidden to participate in the ceremony again if they did not. Some 500 of the tea experts reported for the ten-day training session, bringing their tea utensils with them. The grand tea master of all Japan, Sen-no-Rikyu, revised the ritual at that time, putting the emphasis on purity, peacefulness, reverence, and abstraction. The ceremony itself was simplified so that with a bit of training it could be conducted by anyone interested in participating.

While the tea ceremony has followed the same forms since the 1580s, its surroundings and implements have continuously evolved. The screened-off area of the house that had been used for serving tea to guests gradually became a separate room, often designed with plaster walls rather than a paper divider. Then, many Japanese families followed the suggestion of Sen-no-Rikyu, erecting a whole building, the teahouse, separated from the main house. The teahouse was connected to the main house only by a garden path designed to symbolize a break with the outside world.

The path, called the *roji*, is composed of flat stones placed in a natural, asymmetrical pattern that has been described as regular irregularity. Evergreen plants are usually planted along the *roji* to suggest a forested area, and one or more stone lanterns are placed beside it. A stone water basin may also be placed at a point along the pathway so that guests may rinse their mouths and hands before entering the teahouse. At other times, the fresh cold water represents the water from a mountain spring, which cleanses the guest of worldly dusts. In very cold weather, a pail of hot water may be placed in the basin.

Because a large Japanese garden may contain several pathways leading in different directions, the path to the teahouse may be marked by detainer stones—stones about the size of a fist and wrapped with a cord—that block the alternate pathways. A detainer stone is placed on a stepping stone as a signal that the guest should not continue in that direction.

The entrance to the teahouse is no more than three feet high, thus requiring guests to bow their heads in order to pass through the opening. This also promotes a feeling of humility. And the proper method of entering includes crawling on one's knees, a further mark of humility. Shoes are left outside the entrance. Purists do not wear just any shoes, but specially designed *roji* sandals.

The interior of the teahouse is a square of approximately 3 meters (10 feet) in each direction—in Japanese terms, an area of four and a half mats. There are decorative silk scrolls on the walls and other simple but elegant decorative effects. The tea utensils are kept in an alcove in one corner.

Near the center of the main room is an opening in the floor for a small brazier that is used to heat the tea water. The teahouse also may be equipped with a portable brazier which can be used in one corner of the room or in the area where the tea utensils are kept. Both types of brazier burn charcoal, and it is customary to add incense or special woods that produce a pleasant aroma when the fire is stoked.

The tea utensils include a water jar. The selection of the proper water jar, and certain other utensils, may seem like a ritual in itself. The water jar is usually made of colored enamel pottery, but it is sometimes made of imported bronze or curved wood. Jars originally kept in farm buildings to store seeds are also popular as water jars. The host or hostess may keep several kinds of water jars, including a summer style with a broad opening at the top so that guests can see the water and feel cool.

The tea caddy, a container for keeping powdered tea, also is an important part of the decor. Some tea caddies are spherical; some are cylindrical. Among the favorites are tea caddies shaped like fruits, such as plums or persimmons. A tea caddy may be made of ceramic ware or lacquered wood. Thick powdered teas are usually kept in ceramic tea caddies and thin powdered teas in lacquered wood caddies. The caddy, in turn, is often enclosed in a decorated fabric bag with a drawstring. The tea scoop used for measuring the powdered tea is usually whittled from bamboo or from the wood of a pine or fruit tree. The scoop is kept in a bamboo tube. A tea scoop with a joint carved near the center of its length is an informal type; formal scoops do not have joints.

The teakettle used for the tea ceremony is usually of an almost spherical shape, although one major variation in design is a narrow cylindrical style called a cloud dragon. The main differences are in the size—smaller kettles for portable braziers and larger kettles for floor-mounted braziers—and in the finish—a favorite round kettle style has a rough, hobnail finish called hailstone.

Teabowls—Western-style cups are never used—for the ceremony are of such myriad designs that it would be difficult to create a bowl shape or pattern that does not already exist. Teabowls for summer use generally have a deep lip, while those intended for winter use have a flat lip. Some bowls have a small foot that raises the bottom of the bowl a fraction of an inch above the serving surface. Many prefer a very simple *raku* teabowl of the type used nearly 400 years ago when the *cha no yu* was revised by Sen-no-Rikyu.

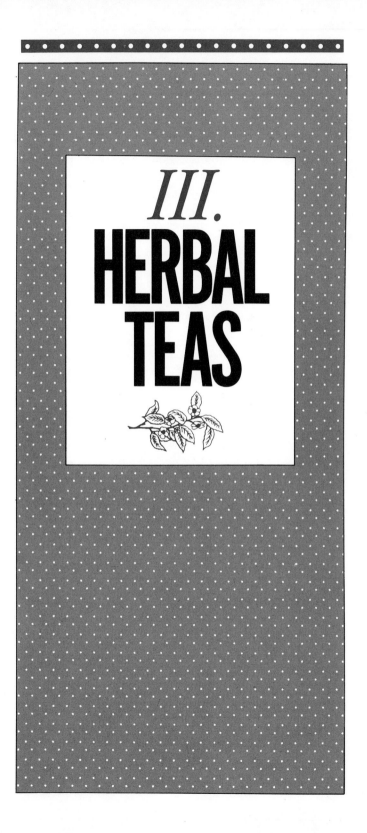

III.
HERBAL
TEAS

1.
Herbal Lore

The world of herbs encompasses every class of vegetation, and it includes every part of the plant, from roots to stems and seeds to the topmost leaves. Many of the substances used to make herbal teas are technically spices. Elderberries and rose hips, for example, are spices rather than herbs, according to purists, because of their high oil content, whereas herbs are presumed to contain little oil. Some experts argue that only the leafy portion of a plant is an herb and all other parts are spices, but bay leaf is regarded as a spice, and garlic has been catalogued as an herb since the first clay tablets and papyri on medications were compiled.

Because many of the most commonly used herbal teas contain an assortment of herbs or spices or both, the attempt to distinguish herbal teas from other beverages prepared by infusions or decoctions from plant leaves, roots, stems, flowers, or seeds is only confusing. Root beer, for example, originally was a fermented beverage made with such ingredients as sassafras, wintergreen, wild cherry bark, allspice, yellow dock, hops, coriander, sugar, and yeast. The original ginger ale was also a fermented beverage containing lemon juice, ginger, and alcohol. The alcohol content of old-time ginger ale was comparable to that of a good European beer or ale.

It makes no sense, then, to rigorously distinguish between herbs and spices, but it should be noted that there are differences between fresh herbs and dried herbs, fresh herbs being decidedly more flavorful. The difference can be as marked as that between a fresh onion slice and dehydrated onion powder. Today, most of us live in a world of instant coffees, instant teas, and dried seasonings, and we are not aware of the intense flavors of fresh wild cherry juice, horseradish, or peppermint. The herbs commonly used in commercial herb teas are dried, unfortunately a necessity since fresh herbs undergo turbulent chemical changes quickly, developing unpalatable flavors. Still, it is possible to grow a few fresh herbs, or pick them in country fields, and make a memorable infusion of herbal teas that have flavor accents you would never experience with dried herbs. For an introduction to herb gathering, see page 127.

The aromas of herbs are unique chemical complexes in

volatile oils. Each herbal has its distinct aroma, occasionally similar but never identical to that of another plant. The oils are volatile because they are designed by nature to evaporate easily into the surrounding atmosphere. They are not created for the pleasure of humans but to attract or repel certain insects.

The aromas and flavors of herbs and spices were very important to people of ancient cultures. In the graves of the ancient Neanderthal people, anthropologists have found traces of flowers buried with the bodies of the Neolithic men and women. The early Egyptians used aromatic spices in the embalming of the dead pharaohs. The Bible contains at least three dozen passing references to herbs, plus many other specific comments about herbs and spices. The Romans used oils scented with fragrant herbs in their baths. Until the Renaissance, when European adventurers began to circumnavigate the world, many of the common aromatic herbs and spices so familiar in kitchens of the Western world today were too rare and expensive for most families. Even the more sophisticated Europeans of the period were uncertain about the sources of the spices that reached their capitals. Because of the complex shipping routes and transshipping of goods by caravans from the Orient, it was commonly believed that many of the spices came from Arabia, which was, in fact, only a transshipment point.

Meals without herbs and spices were quite bland. Medieval documents show that fish was occasionally served with the entrails intact in order to give the meat a bit of flavor. Salt was the main condiment of commerce; a dark substance mixed with impurities of the seawater from which it was manufactured by simple evaporation. Excavations of ancient European homesteads show that weed seeds were commonly used to season foods.

The medieval herbalist's world.

BREWING HERBAL TEAS

To make an infusion of the leaf or flower of a plant, steep it in freshly boiled water for 10 to 15 minutes. A teaspoonful of dried herb per cup of beverage usually will be sufficient, depending upon the herb. Hyssop usually has a flavor intensity that is much greater than summer savory while wild bergamot is about halfway beween hyssop and summer savory in flavor intensity.

Herbal teas made from roots or bark of plants generally need to be steeped in hot water because the essential oils that are the source of aroma and flavor are locked in tougher cellulose plant cells. Some may even require boiling, or decoction, although the preparation time often can be accelerated by pulverizing the plant material to help break down the cell walls before exposing the herb to the boiling water. Fresh herbs have a short shelf life: if you gather more than you can use immediately, dry the remainder. Shred the dried herb and store it in an airtight (and preferably a light-tight) container. Many plant substances undergo chemical changes when exposed to either oxygen or light, which is why many medicines and beverages are sold in containers made of colored glass.

However, most Europeans lived on farms or estates, in close proximity to the wild countryside. Herbs were readily available and every family had at least one member who was expert in the use of herbs for medicines and in foods. Wine, ale, milk, cream and meat broths—as well as water—were combined with appropriate herbs to make foods, drinks, and medication. A cure for constipation, for instance, was garlic simmered in chicken broth.

Parsley was the most popular medieval herb, and both roots and leaves were used. Dandelion, daisy, leeks, lettuce, chives, marigold, red nettle, the roots and leaves of rape and radish, sage, thyme, fennel, and mints were also in common use. Although old recipes often listed mint as the finest herb, they were not always specific as to which of at least 25 varieties of mint was to be used. In fact, herbs were often identified only by local names, which are meaningless in terms of modern botanical classifications. The English at one time even used the leaves of plum trees to make an herbal tea, much as the Chinese began the manufacture of traditional oriental teas from leaves of the tea plant.

In America, herbal teas evolved partly out of European folk knowledge transplanted to the New World. America's first settlers included men and women who had been born during the reign of Queen Elizabeth I. Their knowledge of foods, beverages, and medicines was equal to Europeans', and their comparatively uncivilized circumstances made the knowledge even more useful. Added to the colonists' own lore was information obtained from the American Indians about plants that were not familiar to Europeans.

America's interest in herbal teas received further impetus during the War of Independence, when shipments of China tea were boycotted and substitutes were sought. New Jersey tea was a common substitute. The native Labradore tea was so popular, it was briefly exported to England after hostilities

• •

had ceased. As the frontier was pushed westward from the Atlantic Coast, herbal teas prepared from local plants became an important aspect of daily survival. The germ theory of disease was unknown, but it was general knowledge among frontier people that life expectancy seemed to be related to the use of boiled drinking water. Boiled drinking water itself has so little flavor that even pine needles (actually still used as a substitute for balm of Gilead) were sometimes added to make the potion palatable.

A remarkable number of common garden and wild plants —fresh or dried—can be used in herbal-tea preparation.

2.
A Guide to Herbal Teas

There are countless sources of herbal tea materials. The relatively few included in this listing were selected for their general availability and their comparatively attractive flavor and aroma.

Angelica. A biennial plant that resembles celery with purplish stems, several varieties of angelica grow wild in North America and are cultivated in Europe. In the wild state, angelica is found in bottom-land thickets where the soil is rich and moist. The mature plant is about 2 meters (6 feet) tall with white, yellow, or purplish flowers and green leaves. The leaves may be as much as a meter (3 feet) in length. The botanical name is *Angelica archangelica*, derived from a tradition that the plant flowered on or about the date of the Feast of St. Michael the Archangel. In Medieval Europe the plant was believed to protect a person against the effects of witchcraft, but it is used commercially today as an ingredient in gin, vermouth, and chartreuse.

The herbal tea, which has the flavor of juniper berries, is prepared from seeds of the plant. One teaspoonful of seeds should be added for each cup of boiling water. Angelica has been recommended as a diuretic and for the relief of colic, flatulence, heartburn, and other digestive disorders.

Agrimony. Better known by the common names of cocklebur and sticklewort, agrimony grows wild in fields of North America and Europe. It is a deep green plant less than a meter (3 feet) tall with fine hairs along the stem. The flowers are composed of five golden petals. Agrimony has been used as a folk remedy for centuries, being recommended in Anglo-Saxon England as a treatment for warts, wounds, and snakebite. In the sixteenth century, it was popular as a liver tonic. The leaves and flowers are dried and used in a ratio of one ounce of dried herb to a cup of boiling water. Sweetened with honey, the tea has the strongly aromatic taste of fruit syrup.

Balm. A light green perennial with fragrant, serrated leaves that smell like lemon when crushed. Because of its lemon aroma and flavor, the plant is sometimes identified as lemon balm. Other common names are citronele, honey plant, and cureall. The ancient Greeks reportedly placed sprigs of balm in empty hives to attract swarms of bees. To gather the herb, pick the leaves or the flower buds before the flowers appear. The tea is made using one ounce of dried herb to a pint of hot water. Balm also can be served with lemon and sugar as a cool summer refresher. Balm is said to cure gastrointestinal upsets, headaches, and insomnia, particularly when those complaints are associated with nervous tension. The essential oil of balm is used in the manufacture of cheese, salad dressings, May wine, and aromatic liqueurs.

Balm of Gilead. Not to be confused with common, or lemon, balm, the balm of Gilead is an herb prepared from the leaf buds of certain resinous trees. One form is prepared from the winter buds of the balsam-poplar tree. As a medicinal preparation, a decoction is prepared by boiling a teaspoonful of the buds in a cup of water. The tea has a pungent, resinous flavor. The buds are collected commercially for the manufacture of cough syrups; not surprisingly, the herbal tea can be taken as an expectorant when you have a cough.

Barberry. An ancient European plant that has become established in some areas of North America despite efforts to eradicate it. (Though not pestilential itself, it harbors spores of a disease that can destroy wheat crops.) Barberry is a perennial bush between 1 and 2 meters (3-6 feet) in height, with pale green leaves that emerge above three pronged thorns. The flowers are yellow, a fact that led early doctors to believe the plant was a cure for yellow jaundice. According to the so-called Doctrine of Signatures, the physical traits of plants were supposed to show their values as cures for human diseases.

The root and root-bark are made into a sharp, acidy herbal tea, using one half to one teaspoonful of the dried and powdered bark to a pint of boiling water. The berry juice is made into a fruit drink or a jelly. The curative powers reportedly include relief of symptoms of digestive problems, particularly those of a bilious nature.

Borage. A blue-flowered plant, about 30 centimeters (1 foot) tall, with hairy leaves, borage grows wild and in cultivated gardens in both Europe and North America. The flowers have five petals arranged in a star-shaped pattern. The leaves are used in salads and summer drinks as well as in herbal teas. The fresh leaves have a taste similar to that of the cucumber. The tea is prepared by infusing one ounce of leaves in one pint of boiling water. The summer drink is made by adding lemon and sugar to the infusion, and chilling it. Borage is said to relieve respiratory ailments and to exhilarate the depressed. Pliny advised ancient Romans that borage "always brings joy."

Burdock. A biennial plant that grows wild in Europe and North America, it has one stout stem 1.5 meters (5 feet) high, and large leaves. Flowering stems develop each second year, maturing into globular heads with purple flowers. Tiny hooked points help the plant disperse its seeds because the hooks become attached to any person or animal brushing against the plant. This clinging faculty accounts for the plant's common names: beggar's buttons and love's leaves.

The first-year root is dried and the decoction is made using one ounce of dried root for three cups of water. The tea should be simmered on the stove until the volume of water has been reduced to one pint. The flavor resembles that of asparagus. Ancient herbalists believed burdock had the power to move a woman's uterus if the leaves or seeds were placed on her head or feet. In modern practice, the herbal tea is reputed to work as a diuretic and to produce perspiration.

Camomile. This can be any of several varieties of *chamomila* plant, which are sometimes called bachelor's buttons because of the shape of the flower heads, and which also resemble cone

Clover

flowers. German camomile flowers have a yellow center and white petals. Essential oils in the plant parts produce a soothing, pleasant aroma. In some parts of Europe, camomile plants have been strewn on floors or pathways in order to give the area a good scent.

The herb is made into a pleasant aromatic tea with a slightly bitter but fruity flavor, which is sipped for relief of health problems ranging from toothache to nervousness, from headaches to digestive upsets. The plant's botanical name, *Matricaria*, is derived from the Latin term for womb because it was once used as an herb to treat female troubles.

The English preparation called camomile tea is made from a plant of a different genus and species, sometimes identified as Roman camomile because it was introduced into Great Britain by Romans. It is a branched perennial with white floret flowerheads. The herb contains a strong and bitter essential oil and is made into a tea for digestive disorders. Roman camomile flowers are also used as an ingredient in shampoos. Whichever species you use, you should make the tea by using one teaspoon of the dried herb per cup of boiling water.

Catnip. Not just for cats, catnip, also known as catmint, is an herb that has been used for hundreds of years by humans as an ingredient in refreshing beverages and medications. In all languages, the plant name contains a word fragment that is the local term for cat. The plant grows in gardens and as a wild herb in Europe, Asia, and North America. It is about a meter (3 feet) in height, with greyish-green leaves and flowers that range from white to pink with bright red spots. The leaves and flowers are harvested in August and dried for use in infusions. The herb is used in a ratio of one ounce of dried catnip to a pint of boiling water to make a bitter, minty, horehound-like beverage. The essential oil of catnip is highly volatile, so the herb should not be permitted to steep for more than a few minutes. In the past, catnip tea was mixed with wine for digestive disorders and as a stimulant.

117

● ● ● ● ● ● ● ● ● ● ● ● ● ● ● ● ● ● ●

Chicory. Also known as succory and blue dandelion, it has a light-blue flower and resembles a dandelion when it first appears as a rosette of long, spiked leaves in the spring. As chicory grows during the summer, it develops a stalk of up to a meter (2-3 feet) in height with blue, and sometimes pink, petals that radiate from a round center. Chicory has been used since at least the days of the Romans as a salad green known as wild endive. The dried, ground, and roasted roots are used as a coffee additive or substitute. As an ingredient for herbal tea, a decoction can be made using one ounce of dried, pulverized root to a pint of boiling hot water. It makes a mildly bitter beverage. Chicory has been promoted as an answer to diuretic, laxative, and tonic needs.

Choke Cherry. A wild cherry tree that grows up to 12 meters (40 feet) high along fence lines and in country fields, bearing clusters of white flowers in the spring and clusters of small cherries in autumn. The inner bark of the choke cherry tree is gathered in the autumn and dried. The bark has been used as an ingredient in wild cherry cough syrups.

As an herbal tea, the dried inner bark is used in a proportion of one ounce of bark to a cup of boiling water, producing a liquor with a bitter, fruity flavor. As a medication, choke cherry tea has been used as a sedative, for relief of digestive upsets, and as a general tonic. The juice of the berries has also been used in modern medicines, but mainly to mask the unpleasant taste of other ingredients. The bark and berries contain an acid that may cause adverse effects if ingested in excessive quantities.

Clover. There are many kinds of clover, but the type used as an herb is usually the variety known variously as red clover, sweet clover, or bee-bread. The bee-bread name suggests, quite accurately, that red clover is a popular plant among honey bees. The red flower head of clover is the source of the nectar that makes clover honey. One kind of red clover sports the three leaves, or trifolium, that is the mark of the shamrock. Clover herb teas have been used for treating coughs and as an antispasmodic medication. The tea

Dandelion

sometimes is made by adding an ounce of fresh or dried clover heads to a pint of sugar syrup, which is then boiled and strained. The brew has a fragrant, fresh hay flavor.

Comfrey. Comfrey is a botanical cousin of borage. It is found in rich, moist soil in Europe and in the eastern part of North America. A plant about half a meter (2 feet) in height with broad, hairy leaves and clusters of small, pendulous white to purple flowers, it was known to the ancients as knit bone because it was thought to have the power to heal fractures. The botanical name is derived from a Greek word for uniting separate pieces. An infusion made from comfrey leaves has been used to treat colds, bronchitis, and other respiratory ailments. In Russia, a poultice made of comfrey root has been employed to relieve the symptoms of ulcers and tumors. Dried or fresh leaves are made into a pleasantly bitter tea by infusing one ounce of leaves with a half pint of boiling water.

Dandelion. The English common name of this plant is one of the two names it has in French. Dandelion means, literally, teeth of the lion. The other French name, *pissenlit*, is derived from the reputed diuretic quality of dandelions. The plant is one of the most ancient sources of herbal medication, having been cultivated by the early Egyptian physicians as a source of potions used to treat constipation. Like its distant relative, chicory, the dandelion puts forth tender spring leaves that are used as salad greens. The roots are dried and pulverized as a medicinal herb. Dandelion herbs are bitter and increase in bitterness with age. The medicinal tea is made in a ratio of one teaspoonful of herb to a cup of boiling water, with honey added as necessary to mask the bitter taste.

Elderberry. A wild plant of lowlands and fencelines, the elderberry bush has long been the source of tea, wine, pie, jelly, and ointments for sprains and bruises. It grows both wild and cultivated in Europe and North America. In Europe, the elderberry was associated with witchcraft, so the plant was neither chopped down nor allowed to thrive too close to the house; one was expected to apologize to the plant when it became necessary to prune a branch. According to legend, Judas hanged himself from an elderberry shrub although this seems unlikely in view of the fact that the elderberry seldom reaches a height of more than 3 meters (10 feet). The flowers, leaves, berries, and bark are used for various medicinal purposes, mainly to relieve constipation. The spicy, bitter tea is made from an infusion of dried flowers, mixing in one teaspoon per cup of boiling water. An herbal liqueur, Sambuco Romano, is also made from the plant.

Fennel. An ancient herb that grows in hedgerows and cultivated gardens almost anywhere, provided there is adequate sunlight. The ancient Greeks ate fennel because they believed the plant would give them strength without making them fat; it still is promoted in some areas as a vegetable that can be included in weight-reduction diets. Fennel grows to be about 1.75 meters (6 feet) tall, with yellow flowers that radiate from branches or stems. The fruits and the roots of fennel are made into a decoction of fennel tea. Fennel tastes like a very sweet form of celery. The large stalks, in fact, can be peeled and eaten like celery or used in salads. Fennel seeds are a popular spice. Many medicinal claims have been made for fennel over the centuries; it has been used to cure blindness and to ward off evil spirits. The tea is consumed today as a folk remedy to relieve fluid retention and digestive problems. To make it, you must first bruise the seeds by lightly pounding them. Mix one teaspoon of bruised seeds per cup of boiling water.

Ginseng. One of the world's oldest known herbs, ginseng is described in the Chinese volume, *Shen Nung*, of nearly 5,000 years ago, and according to some herbalists, it is the *pannag* mentioned in the Book of Ezekiel. For most of its history, ginseng was believed

• • • • • • • • • • • • • • • • • • • •

boiling water. The beverage has a pleasant licorice flavor and is claimed to have effects as an aphrodisiac, antispasmodic, heart tonic, stimulant, and digestive aid. Many myths have surrounded the use of ginseng over the centuries, partly because the root sometimes resembles a human body. The Chinese *jen-shen*, or ginseng, translates roughly as essence of man.

Goldenrod. Both a cause and a cure for hay fever according to some herbalists, goldenrod has been served as an herbal tea in Europe for nearly 1,000 years. Plants called goldenrod grow wild in both Europe and North America, though they are not of exactly the same species. A goldenrod plant stands about a meter (3 feet) high with oblong leaves and golden flowerheads, each radiating about eight petals. The leaves have an aroma that hints of anise. The leaves are gathered in summer, dried, and prepared as a tea by infusing one teaspoonful of dried leaves to a cup of boiling water. Medical claims include benefits as a diuretic and stimulant.

Guarana. This is chocolate-colored paste made from the seeds of a liana plant that grows wild in the Amazon basin. The seeds are mixed with both water and a flour prepared from the root of the cassava plant; the mixture is molded into cylinders of guarana paste that are dried, then pulverized into a powder that can be infused as either a hot or cold beverage. Guarana tea contains about three times as much caffeine as strong coffee. A similar beverage, called *yopo*, is made from the bark of a related species of the *Paullinia* genus, that grows in South America, but *yopo* contains about half as much caffeine as guarana. Guarana tea is made in a proportion of one teaspoonful of paste to one pint of hot water.

Horehound. Few herbs in use today have a history as well documented as that of horehound. Horehound, through its botanical name of *Marrubium*, has been identified as marrob, one of the five bitter herbs of the ancient Hebrew Passover ceremonies. It was listed in the Egyptian medical papyri as the seed of Horus. Hippocrates included horehound in his catalog of medical herbs. The modern common name apparently is related to use of the herb during the Renaissance: it was believed that mad dogs would not attack a person whose shoes contained horehound leaves. The plant grows wild in Europe, Africa, Asia, and North America as a half-meter (2 feet) tall perennial, with oval-shaped, veined leaves and small, whitish flowers that seem to grow from the base of the leaf stems. The leaves and flowers are gathered and dried for tea-making. The usual recipe calls for one ounce of dried horehound herb to a pint of boiling water. The tea has a heavy, musky aroma and a bitter taste. The medical value of horehound seems to be mainly in its use as an expectorant taken for coughs and colds, although it is also said to be effective as a stimulant and diuretic.

Hyssop. Hyssop is another of the holy, or sacred, herbs, mentioned several times in the Bible (Psalms, "Purge me with hyssop and I shall be clean.") In ancient times, hyssop was used to treat leprosy. The *Materia Medica* of Dioscorides, compiled in the first century A.D., failed to describe the plant because it was so well known it needed no description. Hyssop is a small, bushy plant, about half a meter (2 feet) in height, with a woody stem near the base and pairs or groups of small narrow leaves spaced at intervals along the branches. Bluish-purple flowers grow on the branches from the points where the leaf stems are attached. All parts of the hyssop plant are used for tea or medications or both, and as potherbs. Hyssop tea—which has a bitter, stringent, minty flavor—is made by gathering the leaves and flowers and drying them for an infusion prepared by adding a teaspoonful of dried hyssop to a cup of boiling hot water. Its main medical value today, as in ancient times, is in the relief of coughs and colds.

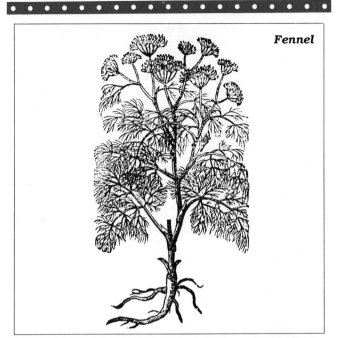

Fennel

Lemon Grass. A lemon-flavored herb used mainly in India as a substitute for real lemons when the aroma and flavor of lemon peel is needed, as in curried dishes. Lemon grass also grows in other tropical regions, such as the West Indies. Lemon grass tea is prepared by making an infusion of one ounce of raw lemon grass to one pint of boiling water. No significant health claims are associated with lemon grass tea.

Lemon Verbena. A small shrub that grows mainly in Latin America but is also found along the Pacific Coast as far north as California, lemon verbena has been cultivated for centuries in European gardens for its penetrating lemon aroma. Like lemon grass, to which it is not related, lemon verbena is often used as an ingredient in foods when a citrus component is needed but real lemons are not available. The raw herb has a much greater flavor intensity than dried lemon verbena, which is the form generally used in the preparation of the herbal tea. It is served in restaurants and bars in Europe as a *tisane* to aid digestion and to relieve nervous tension. The wild plant has angular branches with whorls of three or four leaves at intervals along the stems, and small, pink flowers grow on spikes originating at the base of the leaf whorls. The tea is usually made using one teaspoon of dried leaves per cup of boiling water.

Licorice. An herb that has been used as a source of respiratory and digestive medications since the days of the Ancients. Licorice has been found in the tombs of the pharaohs and is mentioned in Chaucer as one of the *springen herbes*. The licorice plant grows in wet, wild areas of all continents, although it originated in the Mediterranean region. It has deep underground stems and roots, and aerial stems that reach about a meter (3 feet) above the ground. Tiny, pink flowers grow in leaflet cups along the aerial stems. The roots and underground stems are the main source of the herbs used in teas, medicines, and confections.

The tea is a decoction made using the root and underground stem, having a flavor more acrid and bitter than licorice candy, but pleasant enough. Mix one teaspoon of powdered root per cup of boiling water. In Europe, dried licorice is prepared in an infusion with milk for use as a remedy in respiratory tract infections. True licorice is not related to the wild licorice plant, also known as spikenard or pigeon weed, that is common in wooded areas of the eastern United States.

Mallow. The original source of the mucilaginous paste used in the manufacture of marshmallow, the mallow is another of the herbs that was brought from Europe to North America during settlement of the Colonies. It is a perennial plant that grows in marshland, and has fleshy roots that are white on the outside and yellow on the inside. The stem bears large, serrated leaves and flowers that consist of five pinkish petals radiating from the base of the stamen. The root, which is nearly 60 percent starch and pectin, is used as the mallow herb. The carbohydrates give mallow a cloyingly sweet taste. The tea can be made from the roots or the leaves, by steeping three teaspoons of chopped root or one and a half teaspoons of dried leaves for eight hours in one cup of cold water. The liquid should be strained and thoroughly heated before you drink it.

Marigold. The botanical name of the plant is *Calendula* because of a traditional belief that it can be seen in flower on the *calends*, or first day, of each month of the year. It is also known as the marybud because of a legend that the flower was worn by the Mother of Jesus. The marigold is believed to have originated in India, where it is the sacred flower of the Hindus, but it has spread to other parts of the world where it often grows wild. It is also cultivated for its beauty and as the ingredient for a folk remedy. The plant stands about 45 centimeters (18 inches) tall, bearing a flowerhead nearly 8 centimeters (3 inches) across with a mass of yellow-orange petals. The petals are dried and infused to make a hot beverage. Because the taste resembles saffron, it is a saffron substitute. The petals also have been used in broths, in salads, and in the manufacture of marigold cheese. As a folk remedy, the marigold essence has been used to treat menstrual disorders, anemia, and respiratory complaints. To make the tea, use one teaspoon of dried petals per cup of boiling water.

Maté. Also known as yerba mate and Paraguay tea, maté is an herb prepared from the leaves of a South American evergreen shrub, *Ilex paraguayensis*, a relative of common holly. The leaves are oval and about 16 centimeters (6 inches) long. Flowers of the plant are small and white. The fruit appears as small clusters of tiny red berries growing close to the stems of the plant. Like guarana and *yopo*, maté is rich in caffeine and was used as a caffeine beverage source by the native population of Latin America centuries before the European settlers arrived to establish coffee plantations. Maté leaves are processed somewhat like tea leaves. The tips of the branches are cut just before the leaves reach full growth and the leaves are dried over fires, changing the chemistry of the raw resins and reducing the moisture content. The dried, toasted leaves are threshed, sifted, and allowed to age in order to enhance their flavor. The caffeine content of maté is comparable to that of a mild *arabica* coffee.

The tea is prepared from the dried leaves, using one teaspoon of dried leaves per cup of boiling water. The aroma and flavor are of toasted leaves. The traditional native procedure involves making a cold-water infusion in a small bowl and inserting a hollow tube or straw into the bowl, through which the tea is sipped. Some of the tubes are made of silver with a perforated strainer at the bottom to prevent the maté leaf particles from being sucked up through the tube. The bowl, called a *cuya*, and the tube, the *bombilla*, are used in ceremonies at which participants take turns sipping maté through the silver straw.

Meadowsweet. Also known as meadwort and queen of the meadows, this herb was a favorite of the druids as a source for remedies and an ingredient in foods and beverages. The tea has a sweet and slightly astringent taste. Meadowsweet was at one time used in the production of mead and still is a component of an herbal beer made with agrimony, dandelions, and yeast. It grows to a height of about a meter (3 feet). Meadowsweet grows wild in Europe and Asia, a perennial with large downy leaves and whitish-yellow flowers that grow in clusters on branching stems. The flowers and leaves are gathered and dried for use as an herbal tea, as well as in the manufacture of medicines. To make tea, one ounce of dried herb is added to one pint of boiling water. Meadowsweet is relatively harmless, so the entire flowering plant is sometimes used in the preparation of folk remedies. It is reputed to have beneficial effects for persons suffering from rheumatic complaints and also is used as a diuretic and an astringent. Meadowsweet was a favorite of Queen Elizabeth I, who used it as a strewing herb to carpet the floors of her chambers.

Mint. Probably the oldest and largest family of herbs, more than 2,000 known species of mint have been recorded in a history that dates back to the earliest traces of medical prescriptions. The family really includes hyssop and horehound, bergamot and bee to grow only in the Orient, but in the early eighteenth century a missionary to the American Indians discovered the same plant growing in Canada. For the next 150 years, many American hunters and trappers on the frontier made more money by digging up ginseng roots than by selling furs. American merchants began to sell ginseng to the Chinese, in exchange for silks and tea. The ginseng hunters included Daniel Boone, according to records of a Philadelphia merchant of the era.

Ginseng, which grows in cool, wooded areas, has upright stems with three leaves and with red fruit on each stem. The root of ginseng is made into a tea by chopping it into fine pieces and making a decoction of a quarter of an ounce of root to a quart of

Meadowsweet

balm, sage and summer savory, all listed separately in this guide. The true mints, identified by the botanical genus *Mentha*, are much more limited in number, and the better-known types are peppermint and spearmint.

Peppermint is believed to be a hybrid species that evolved long ago from spearmint and watermint. However, peppermint has been around so long its genealogy is obscure. It reportedly was used as a strewing herb by the ancient Hebrews, and it has been found in 3,000-year-old Egyptian tombs. The Japanese were growing it 2,000 years ago as a source of menthol, while first-century Romans served it with their meat dishes. The peppermint plant grows as a square-stemmed flower with a creeping rootstock. Tiny trumpet-shaped pink flowers appear at the end of each stem in a false whorl. It grows wild in Europe and North America, and is cultivated for commercial and domestic purposes. Peppermint is a primary ingredient in remedies used for the relief of gastrointestinal disorders, headaches, and local aches and pains. Because of its bright, pungent flavor, peppermint also is used to mask the unpalatable taste of some medicines. Peppermint tea is made from both the leaves and flowers, infusing one teaspoonful of the herb with one cup of water. When the tea is taken as a cold beverage, the menthol content produces a pleasantly chilling taste sensation.

Spearmint has a sharper flavor and lacks the cooling aftertaste of peppermint. The spearmint plant, ancestor of the peppermint plant, not surprisingly resembles its descendant closely. The main clues in making identification are the plant colors, which are darker in peppermint plants, and the leaves, which show a greater proliferation of hair, or down, in the peppermint variety. Spearmint tea is prepared with one ounce of dried leaf to a pint of boiling water, and sweetened to taste.

Mullein. A tall, spiky plant with yellow flowers and a variety of common names including candleflower, hightaper, Aaron's rod, and lungwort. The word fragment, *wort*, is derived from an ancient Saxon term for a medicinal herb and is a clue that the plant was used in medieval times for the treatment of respiratory ailments. Actually, mullein was known in ancient Rome for its unexplained ability to help preserve foods wrapped in its leaves. Mullein was imported from Europe where, aside from its value as a medicinal herb, it also was planted in gardens in the belief that the 2-meter-high (7 feet) grayish stalks would frighten demons of the night. North American Indians discovered that mullein leaves mixed with ordinary tobacco leaves produced a psychogenic smoke that relaxed the disturbed mind. Mullein leaves, and occasionally the flowers, are dried and pulverized to make an herb for a bittersweet tea, in the ratio of one ounce of herb to a pint of boiling water. Mullein is used today, as in Medieval Europe, to provide relief of respiratory distress. Before the introduction of miracle drugs for the cure of tuberculosis, patients were often given an infusion of mullein boiled in milk.

Nettle. The stinging nettle is a botanical paradox. Its needlelike hairs contain a poison that produces a painful sting when the plant is touched, but preparations made from the plant contain the remedy for its own sting. Because of the irritation of the poison, the plant has been used to stimulate blood circulation near the skin to relieve rheumatic complaints. Roman soldiers reportedly used nettle plants for a similar reason: increasing blood circulation in the extremities made it possible to tolerate cold-weather campaigns. The paradox of the nettle is resolved by boiling or drying the leaves, which causes the chemical changes necessary to eliminate the toxic effect. Both the seeds and the boiled leaves can be used to make an infusion of nettle tea, which has a taste resembling mildly salted spinach. Again, mixing one teaspoon of herb per cup of water will produce the best results.

Raspberry

Medical claims made for nettle have varied through history. In the third century B.C., nettle was used to treat snakebite and scorpion stings; a century later, nettle was recommended as an antidote for hemlock or toadstool poisoning. In recent centuries, the herb, consumed as a wine, beer, or tea, has been recommended for tuberculosis, asthma, and other respiratory diseases.

Raspberry. A wild member of the rose family, it is found along fencelines and in wooded areas of Europe, Asia, and North America. The plant appears as a thorned cane about 2 meters (6 feet) in height, with white to pink flowers that change during the summer into small, conical fruits. The fruits are usually red but may vary in shade according to differences in species and varieties. The leaves contain tannin, which produces an astringent but refreshing and soothing taste when made into an infusion by mixing one ounce of leaves with one pint of boiling water. The plant is rich in minerals and vitamins, which may account for its assorted health effects when used in folk remedies. It is also claimed that the raspberry contains a substance that relieves certain difficulties of the female reproductive organs.

Rose Hips. Rose hip tea with honey was recommended in *Bancke's Herbal* of 1525 for the "feeble, sick, phlegmatic, melancholy, and choleric" person, even though the reason for the health benefit of the beverage was not discovered until recently. Now it is known that one ounce of rose hips contains about as much vitamin C as a whole crate of fresh oranges. The rose hip, or hep, is the more or less spherical pod that is the fruit of the rose plant. During World War II, rose hip jelly was an important substitute for citrus fruits while international shipping lanes were disrupted.

Rose hips are dried and pulverized to make a tea herb. The flavor is mildly sweet and tangy; the bitterness of the raw rose hip is diminished when used in a hot drink. The tea is best made by steeping one teaspoon of sliced rose hips in a cup of cold water for 12 hours. The strained liquid is then heated before it is drunk. Acidity varies with the variety of rose that produced the hips, and wild rose hips are usually more flavorful than the hips of any

125

domesticated rose plants. Honey is often added to infusions or decoctions of rose hips.

Sage. Sage is a member of the large mint family whose botanical genus is *Salvia*, derived from the Latin word for healing. During the Middle Ages, diners were advised to wash their hands in sage water before touching their food. A Medieval motto was, "Why should a man die whilst sage grows in his garden?" There are 500 different varieties of sage, but the kind most commonly used in food and tea preparation is a shrubby plant that grows to a height of about half a meter (2 feet), with a woody base and purple flowers on terminal spikes. The aromatic leaves, which contain an essential oil that has a tonic and digestive effect, is the part of the plant used as an herb. The leaves are dried for use in tea, which is made with one teaspoonful of dried sage to a cup of water. The sage leaves—which have a bitter, pungent flavor comparable in intensity to oregano and an aroma of camphor—are also used in food preparation when a bit of green color is needed. It should be noted that the sage that is processed as an herb is not related to the sagebrush of the southwestern United States.

Yarrow. The botanical name of yarrow includes the species designation, *millefolium*, or thousand flowers, which describes rather accurately the appearance of the herb. Yarrow is a member of the daisy family and the myriad white to pink flower heads on the stems resemble miniature daisies. Yarrow also seems to have a myriad common names, including nose-bleed, old man's pepper, and woundwort. Old man's pepper refers to yarrow's peppery, pungent aroma; nose-bleed to its ability to induce nosebleeds; and woundwort to its reputed ability to stop bleeding. The flowers are gathered in August and dried for use as an herb. The tea, pleasantly bitter in aroma and flavor, is made in a proportion of one ounce of herb to one pint of boiling water. It has been used as a folk remedy for boils, hemorrhoids, and ulcers, among other disorders.

BLENDING HERBAL TEA

Just as coffee and tea contribute flavors that often blend pleasurably with aromas, flavors, and textures of other foods and beverages, so the flavors of unblended herbal teas often become more palatable when they are blended. Herbal beverages have inherent flavor qualities that sometimes need to be modified with other taste sensations or, in some cases, can be used to modify the flavor of another herb. Peppermint, spearmint, and wild cherry, for example, have such dominant flavors that their greatest value may be in their ability to improve the taste of another herb that has greater health effects but a bland or uninteresting taste.

If you are less adventurous, you can buy some blends in premixed packages from commercial herbal tea companies. Otherwise, you may enjoy blending your own, experimentally, until you find the proportions you like best. The combinations listed on the following page can guide your purchases or experiments.

SUGGESTED COMBINATIONS

Angelica	Balm, Rhubarb
Agrimony	Licorice, Lemon
Balm	Almond, Honey, Apple
Balm of Gilead	Mint, Wild Cherry
Barberry	Honey
Borage	Lemon, Honey
Burdock	Mint
Camomile	Fennel, Sage
Catnip	Red Wine, Honey
Chicory	Balm, Lemon, Mint
Choke Cherry	Rose Hips, Burdock
Clover	Balm, Mint
Comfrey	Honey, Lemon
Dandelion	Agrimony, Burdock, Lemon
Elderberry	Honey, Mint
Fennel	Camomile, Burdock
Ginseng	Chicory, Licorice, Raspberry
Goldenrod	Rose Hips, Dandelion
Guarana	Lemon Grass, Peppermint
Horehound	Licorice, Raspberry
Hyssop	Borage, Nettle, Sage
Lemon Grass	Chicory, Rose Hips
Lemon Verbena	Comfrey, Raspberry, Rose Hips
Licorice	Ginseng, Dandelion, Chicory
Mallow	Burdock, Rose Hips
Marigold	Lemon Verbena, Raspberry
Mate	Regular Black Tea, Chicory
Meadowsweet	Lemon Verbena, Mint
Mint	Camomile, Rose Hips, Dandelion
Mullein	Lemon Grass, Mint
Nettle	Lemon, Wild Cherry
Raspberry	Camomile, Goldenrod, Rose Hips
Rose Hips	Lemon Verbena, Fennel, Mint, Raspberry
Sage	Lemon Grass, Mint
Yarrow	Licorice, Mint

HERB HUNTERS GUIDE

If you live in China or Sri Lanka or India, one of the herbs you can gather from local shrubs is *Camellia sinensis*, otherwise known as tea. In Brazil or Ethiopia, you probably could find the seeds of an evergreen called *Coffea arabica*, an herb used to prepare a tea most of the world calls coffee. An herb that formerly grew wild throughout much of North America, *Panax quinquefolius*, or American ginseng, was once in such demand that the first United States commercial sailing ship in 1784 carried a cargo of *Panax quinquefolius* to China to trade for a cargo of *Camellia sinensis!*

For many people, an herb is a plant material with an exotic botanical name that grows somewhere else. Actually, most of us live surrounded by herbs; few individuals even in large cities are beyond easy walking distance of at least a few herbal varieties. As John Lust notes in his handy treatise, *The Herb Book* (Bantam Books, 1974), the late Euell Gibbons

127

once found a dozen medicinal and edible herbs growing in the median of a San Francisco street. He could identify them because he had acquired the knowledge once possessed by most of our ancestors but forgotten by us.

Although many herbs, including ginseng, can be found in more than one part of the world, quite a few prefer certain regions or climates. Europeans who migrated to North America often transplanted their favorite herbs to their new homesites, just as migrating Chinese transplanted their teas to Taiwan. Other herbs refused to make the transition. Obviously, the tea herbs that do not grow in your own region must be obtained through mail-order or specialty stores. You may well want to gather the rest of them yourself.

It is wise to begin by studying one of the many herbal handbooks available in paperback or hardbound form, such as the John Lust paperback mentioned above. Local officials of agricultural agencies or nature organizations also can contribute guidance about herbs found in your own area. For the novice, particularly, it is most important to be able to make a positive identification of a plant before beginning to harvest his own herbs.

A few light handtools and a number of plastic bags with labels are sufficient equipment for a day of herb hunting in

HERBAL MEDICINE

Herbal medicines are probably not as effective as their ardent devotees claim, nor as useless as some doctors believe. A report of the U.S. Department of Health and Human Services suggests that herbal infusions have fallen into disrepute among the doctors of the industrialized countries because tests of their effectiveness were improperly performed. Western scientists, says the study, made the mistake of analyzing the herbs to discover their chemical components, then studying the components in isolation. They failed to consider the combined effects of varying combinations of herbs. Oriental herb doctors, it turns out, rarely use one herb alone, and when they do, they certainly don't isolate its components.

Bad translation has also been a hindrance to the study of oriental herb medicine. A certain Chinese character, for instance, has been translated as spleen. Doctors tested medicines supposed to act on the spleen and found them ineffective. It happens, however, that the idiogram does not mean spleen at all; rather, it refers to the whole gastrointestinal tract. Proving that the herb had no effect on that much more complicated part of the body has not been so easy.

In fact, herbal principles are used in numerous modern medications. The caffeine of coffee, tea, cola, and cocoa is used in medications as a central nervous system stimulant and for the treatment of migraine headaches. Theophyline, a chemical cousin of caffein found in tea, is used in asthma medications. Theobromine, a chemical in cocoa, acts as a heart stimulant and a diuretic in some modern medicines. Oil of wintergreen, used as a counter-irritant by doctors, and ginger, used to control gastrointestinal disorders, are also common ingredients in soft drinks. Cinnamon oil, peppermint oil, mustard seed, and cloves are all used in scientifically prepared medicines, though most of us are more familiar with their uses in foods, teas, and candies. The herbal-medicine issue, then, is far from closed.

the countryside. The hand tools should include a small folding spade for digging rootstocks, a sharp knife, and a small saw for cutting stems. The knife is sufficient for most cutting, but a saw of the type that consists of a thin flexible blade with a finger ring at each end is worth the few extra ounces it adds to your pack.

Study the herbal handbooks before starting out on an herb-hunting trek, or better yet, carry one of the handbooks in your pack to help identify the plants. You will find that in many instances, there are certain specific times of the season when leaves or flowers or other parts must be collected. For most herbs, there are even certain times of the day when the plants should be harvested, usually in the early morning before the dew has evaporated.

Certain varieties of plants may be protected by law as endangered species, putting them beyond the hunter's reach. Even a plant that is not on the endangered list should not be mutilated in order to obtain a few flowers, leaves, or berries.

Be wary of the condition of the plant materials you collect. Avoid herbals that show signs of fungus, insect infestation, or discoloration. Also, the plant materials you collect may have been treated with herbicides, pesticides, or related toxic substances. If you plan to harvest in an area where pesticides are used, try to plan your herb-hunting expedition soon after a good rainstorm. The rain washes off most chemicals. Wash the herb well again, after bringing it home.

Not all herbs are intended to be used in fresh condition. Many, like tea leaves, need to be dried before being made into a beverage infusion. The herbal-tea listings in this book offer guidance regarding the best way to use a particular root, leaf, flower, or fruit, but you may also consult the sources listed below.

For further reading:

Bianchi, Francesco, and Corbetta, Francesco. *Health Plants of the World*. New York: Newsweek Books, 1977. (London: Cassell & Collier Macmillan, 1977.)

Hendrick, U.P. *Sturtevant's Edible Plants of the World*. New York: Dover, 1972.

Lowenfeld, Claire, and Back, Philippa. *The Complete Book of Herbs and Spices*. Boston: Little, Brown, 1974.

Lust, John. *The Herb Book*. New York: Bantam, 1974.

Scully, Virginia. *A Treasury of American Indian Herbs*. New York: Crown, 1970.

Note: Asterisk indicates that shop takes mail order. All stores carry coffees and teas, unless otherwise noted.

UNITED STATES AND CANADA

*American Tea, Coffee and Spice Company, 1511 Champa Street, Denver, CO 80202

*Aphrodisia Products, 28 Carmine Street, New York, NY 10014. Herbal teas only.

Barzula Torrefazione, 669 College, Toronto, Ontario

*Bon Appetit, 213 South 17th Street, Philadelphia, PA 19103. Coffee only.

Caffe Brasiliano, 850 Dundas W., Toronto, Ontario

*Caravansary, 2263 Chestnut Street, San Francisco, CA 94123

*Casa Moneo, 210 West 14th Street, New York, NY 10011. Coffee and mate.

*Celestial Seasonings, P.O. Box 4367, Boulder, CO 80302. Herbal teas only.

*The Coffee Bean, Burlington Mall, 777 Guelph Line, Burlington, Ontario

*The Coffee Bean, 13020-D San Vincente Blvd., Los Angeles, CA 90049

*The Coffee Bean Company, 2465 Hillyard Street, Eugene, OR 97405

The Coffee Bean Inc., 217 King Street, Alexandria, VI 22314

The Coffee Connection, 36 Boylston Street, Cambridge, MA 02138

The Coffee Gallery, 40 Green Street, Northampton, MA 01060

The Coffee Mill, 6435 Westheimer, Houston, TX 77057

Coffees of the World, 1230 Yonge Street, Toronto, Ontario. Write for other locations.

*The Coffee Trader, 2619 North Downer Avenue, Milwaukee, WI 53211

The Coffee Tree, 69 Yorkville, Toronto, Ontario

Dinah's Cupboard, 50 Cumberland, Toronto, Ontario

*East India Tea and Coffee Company, 1481 3rd Street, San Francisco, CA 94107

*Empire Coffee and Tea Company, 486 Ninth Avenue, New York, NY 10018

*First Colony Coffee and Tea Company, P.O. Box 11005, Norfolk, VA 23517

*Flavorworld, 622 Ann Street, New Orleans, LA 70116

Freed, Teller and Freed, 1326 Polk Street, San Francisco, CA

*Gertrude H. Ford Tea Company, P.O. Box 3407, 110 Dutchess Turnpike, Poughkeepsie, NY 12603

Gillies' Coffee Company, 1484 Third Avenue, New York, NY 10028

*Grace Tea Company, Ltd., 799 Broadway, New York, NY 10003. Tea only.

Graffeo Coffee House, 733 Columbus Avenue, San Francisco, CA Coffee only.

The Great Canadian Coffee Company, 77 McCaul, Toronto, Ontario.

*Hilltop Herb Farm, P.O. Box 866, Cleveland, TX 77327. Herbal teas only.

*Homecrafts, 111 Stratford Center, Winston-Salem, NC 27104

*House of Yemen East, 370 Third Avenue, New York, NY 10016

*The Kobos Company, 533 S.W. Macadam, Portland, OR 97201

*Lhasa Karnak Herb Company, 2482 Telegraph Avenue, Berkeley, CA 94704. Herbal teas only.

McNulty's Tea & Coffee Company, 109 Christopher Street, New York, NY 10014

*Murchie's Tea and Coffee Ltd. 1008 Robson Street, Vancouver, British Colombia

*Northwestern Coffee Mills, 217 North Broadway, Milwaukee, WI 53202

Old Georgetown Coffee House, 1330 Wisconsin Avenue, Washington, DC 20007

*The Pannikin, 1296 Prospect Street, LaJolla, CA 92037

*Paprikas Weiss, 1546 Second Avenue, New York, NY 10028

Peet's Coffee, Tea & Spices Company, 2124 Vine Street, Berkeley, CA 94708

*Rocky Hollow Herb Farm, R.D. 2, Box 215, Lake Wallkill Road, Sussex, NJ 07461. Herbal teas only.

*M. Rohrs, 1692 Second Avenue, New York, NY 10028

*Schapira Coffee Company, 117 West 10th Street, New York, NY 10011

*Starbucks Coffee Company, 2000 Western Avenue, Seattle, WA 98121

M.E. Swing Company, 1013 E Street N.W. Washington, DC 20004

*Zabar's, 2245 Broadway, New York, NY 10024

UNITED KINGDOM

Algerian Coffee Stores Ltd. 52 Old Compton Street, Soho, London W1

J. Allan Braithwaite, 6 Castle Street, Dundee

S.D. Bell & Co. Ltd. 516 Upper Newtownards Road, Belfast

Bewley's Cafe, 78-79 Grafton Street, Dublin

*Coffee Roast Ltd. 43 Carfax, Horsham

*The Coffee Shop, 58 King Street, Cambridge

Collinson's, John Street Market, Bradford

Costa Coffee Boutique, 324 Vauxhall Bridge Road, Victoria, SW1

N.H. Creber Ltd. 48 Brook Street, Tavistock

The Drury Tea & Coffee Co. Ltd. 3 New Row, St. Martin's Lane, WC2

Fazzi Brothers, 232 Clyde Street, Glasgow

L. Fern & Co. Unit 7, The Market, Covent Garden, WC2

Gillards, 14 Broad Street, Bath

The Good Taste Shop, 12 St Giles Square, Northampton

H. Gunton, 81-83 Crouch Street, Colchester

Harrods, Brompton Road, Knightsbridge, SW1

*H.R. Higgins (Coffee Man) Ltd. 42 South Molton Street, W1

Importers, 115 High Street, Bromley

James Stevenson, 49 53 King Street, Castle Douglas

John Watt & Son, 11 Bank Street, Carlisle

Keiths, 22 Castles Hill, Cirensester

E.W. King & Son., 8 Market Hall, Sidbury

Knightsbridge Coffee Centre, 248 Fulham Road, SW10

Lewis & Cooper Ltd. Market Place, Northallerton

Maher's of Cork, 29-31 Marlborough Street, Cork

Markus Coffee, 13 Connaught Street, Bayswater, W2

*Monmouth Coffee House, 27 Monmouth Street, Covent Garden, WC2

Ough & Sons Ltd. 10 Market Street, Carlisle

E. Parsons (Tea & Coffee Ltd.) 31-32 High East Street, Dorchester

Rackstraws of North Walsham, 5 Market Street, North Walsham

Robertsons Ltd., 17 Church Street, Reigate

Richmond Tea & Coffee Co. 9 Hill Rise, Richmond

Seed's Coffee House, Dane Road, Seaford

*Sunleaf Tea & Coffee Co. 72 Sheen Road, Richmond

Three Star Products & Camden Coffee Shop, 11 Delancey Street, Camden Town, NW1

Villa Fern, 5 Montpelier Vale, Blackheath, SE3

Wheatsheaf, 59c High Street, Great Missenden

Whittard & Co. Ltd. 111 Fulham Road, South Kensington, SW3

*Wilkinsons, 49 Magdalen Street, Norwich

Index